A NEW WINDMILL BOOK OF FICTION AND NON-FICTION

Taking Off!

STEVE BARLOW
AND STEVE SKIDMORE

Heinemann
New Windmills

Heinemann Educational Publishers
Halley Court, Jordan Hill, Oxford OX2 8EJ
A division of Reed Educational and Professional Publishing Ltd

OXFORD MELBOURNE AUCKLAND
JOHANNESBURG BLANTYRE GABORONE
IBADAN PORTSMOUTH NH (USA) CHICAGO

04 03 02 01 00
10 9 8 7 6 5 4 3 2 1

ISBN 0 435 12516 8

Acknowledgements
The Editors and Publishers should like to thank the following for permission to use copyright material:
Morris Gleitzman for 'Olympic Marathon' taken from 'Just What I Always Wanted'; Orion Publishing
Group Limited, for 'Seeing Red' by Alan Durant; Andre Deutsch Limited for the extract from 'My 1998
World Cup Story' by Glenn Hoddle; Penguin Books Limited for the extract from (text and illustrations
pages 10–15) 'Nutty Footy Book' by Martin Chatterton (Puffin 1994) Copyright © Martin Chatterton
1994; Dragon's Word Limited for the extract 'Magic Johnson' from '100 Greatest Sports Champions' by
Donald Somerville. Copyright © Dragon's World Limited 1997; Thomas Nelson & Sons Limited for
'Seventeen Oranges' by Bill Naughton, taken from 'Goalkeeper's Revenge' by Bill Naughton;
HarperCollins Publishers (text) and George Hollingworth (illustration) for the extract from 'The Lost
Diary of Shakespeare's Ghost Writer' by Steve Barlow and Steve Skidmore; Cherrytree Press Limited for
the extract from 'Guy Fawkes' by Leon Ashworth; The Watts Publishing Group Limited, 96 Leonard
Street, London EC2A 4XD for the extract adapted from 'Viewpoints: A Punishment to fit the Crime' by
Alison Cooper, first published in the UK by Franklin Watts in 1996; Aladdin Books Limited for the extract
from 'Fact and Fiction: Bandits and Outlaws' by Stewart Ross; Dragon's World Limited for the extract
'Mary Read and Anne Bonny' from '100 Greatest Tyrants' by Andrew Langley. Copyright © Dragon's
World Limited 1996; Jennifer Luithlen Agency for 'The Lex Files' by Robet Swindells, taken from 'Just What I
Always Wanted', published by Collins Picture Lions; A.P. Watt Limited on behalf of Helen Dunmore for,
'The Airman's Sixpence' by Helen Dunmore, taken from 'Incredibly Creepy Stories' ed by Tony
Bradman, published by Tranworld; Laurence Pollinger Limited for 'Leaving Sarajevo' by Judith
Hemington, taken from 'Gripping War Stories' published by Doubleday; Random House UK Limited for
the extract from 'Ethel and Ernest' by Raymond Briggs, published by Jonathan Cape; Pavillion Books for
the extract from 'Farm Boy' by Michael Morpurgo; Penguin Australia Limited for 'Moonies' by Paul
Jennings, taken from 'Undone', published by Penguin Australia Limited; Oxford University Press for
'Dare You' by Robert Scott, taken from 'The Oxford Book of Scary Tales'; African Adrenalin.co.za for
'Bungee Jumping From Victoria Falls Bridge'; Penguin Australia Limited for 'Spaghetti Pig-Out' by Paul
Jennings, taken from 'Uncanny' published by Penguin Australia Limited; Brian Patten c/o Rogers,
Coleridge and White Limited, 20 Powis Mews, London W11 1YN for 'At The Zoo' by Brian Patten, taken
from 'Grizzelda Frizzle'. Copyright © Brian Patten 1992; Scholastic Limited for the extract adapted from
'Seriously Weird True Stories 2' by Hervie Brennan; Oxford University Press for the extract from 'How to
Build a Time Machine' by Hazel Richardson (text and illustrations excluding layout; from pages 57–61 of
'How to Build a Time Machine' by Hazel Richardson; Ginn & Co for the extracts from 'Gruesome Urban
Myths' by Rick Glanvill and Phil Healey; The Nottingham Evening Post for the extracts taken from
'Nottingham Evening Post'.

The Publishers have made every effort to trace the copyright holders, but if they have inadvertently
overlooked any, they will be pleased to make the necessary arrangements at the first opportunity.

Cover by Corbis/ Paul A Souders
Designed and produced by The Point
Illustrations by Jackie Hill at 320 Design; page 19 – Hashim Akib; page 54 – Philip Hood;
page 62 – David Hopkins; page 81 – Hashim Akib; page 162 – Tony Watson.
Typeset by ⋆ Tek-Art, Croydon, Surrey
Printed and bound in the United Kingdom by Clays Ltd, St Ives plc

Contents

Introduction for Teachers

Taking Off! is a collection of fiction and non-fiction texts primarily intended for Key Stage 3 students who are working towards National Curriculum Level 4. Our emphasis has been to choose a range of text types that will engage and enthuse students. We have also been aware that students need work of high quality and high interest.

Our fiction choices include well-known and established children's authors such as Robert Swindells, Morris Gleitzman and Raymond Briggs. The non-fiction texts include a range of forms as set down by the National Curriculum: autobiography, journals, newspaper articles, adverts and Internet information.

In order to give the collection a manageable structure we have organised the texts into thematic sections: 'Good Sport, Bad Sport', 'Crime', 'War', 'Do You Dare?', and 'Weird!' – choices that students will enjoy.

A variety of activities, including use of ICT, follow each section. They are designed to consolidate the skills outlined in the National Literacy Strategy objectives at Key Stage 3, mostly at text level, but include some word and sentence level coverage where appropriate. Activities are also provided for comparing texts within sections.

We trust that you will find this collection stimulating and enjoyable and hope that it will encourage your students to 'take off' with their reading!

Steve Barlow and Steve Skidmore

Introduction for Students

The phone rang. It was Heinemann, the publishers.

'Oi! Barlow and Skidmore!' they said. *'Get a load of brilliant stories and interesting non-fiction together, so students can have fun reading and we'll publish it!'*

Oh, all right – they didn't say it exactly like that, but that's what they meant. Okay, we thought, 'sounds good – we'll do it!' So we hurried off to our bookshelves and the library and the Internet to begin our search. We spent hours and hours finding stories and articles that we thought you'd enjoy before we finally chose the material in this book.

Some of the fiction we chose will make you laugh, some will give you the creeps, some will make you think and some will make you say 'No way!'

We also realised that non-fiction is sometimes stranger than fiction! Can a person suddenly burst into flames? Did a tomato seed really grow into a child's brain? Read the extracts and make up your own minds.

You can also find out how to eat spaghetti backwards, what Glenn Hoddle thought about David Beckham being sent off in the 1998 World Cup and why people might throw themselves off a bridge! There are stories of war and crime and ghosts and dares and what happens when a new pupil bares his bottom at the School Principal and . . . well, there's lots more . . .

So start turning those pages and get reading!

Ready for take off? 3 – 2 – 1 . . .

Enjoy!

Steve Barlow and Steve Skidmore

Section 1
Good Sport, Bad Sport

Olympic Marathon
Morris Gleitzman

Sport-mad dad awards his family Olympic medals for events such as teeth-cleaning and nose-picking! But will he go too far?

The Twenty-seventh Summer Olympics arrive in Australia – four years early!

'Manchester,' I pleaded softly. 'Please, let it be Manchester.'

Hoppy, my pet wallaby, stared at me as if I was mad, but I didn't care.

'Manchester,' I moaned desperately, 'or Beijing.'

I held my breath.

Hoppy held his.

The bloke on the telly announced that the Olympic Games in the year 2000 had been awarded to . . . Sydney.

Australia went bananas.

In our lounge room and across our town and up and down the state and right round the country people leapt out of their chairs and whooped with joy and hugged each other and their pets.

All except me.

I just sat there and watched Dad try to do a delighted cartwheel and crash into the electric bug zapper.

'Here we go,' I muttered to Hoppy. 'We're cactus, now.'

It started that evening.

I was drying up after tea when I heard Dad's voice behind me.

'A superb effort from the eleven-year-old,' he said. 'Look at that wiping action. This could be his personal best on the saucepan with lid.'

I sighed.

OK, Dad does a pretty good sports commentator's voice for an abattoir worker, but all I could think of was the one thousand nine hundred and twenty-seven days to go till the Sydney Olympics.

'But wait!' yelled Dad. 'Look at this burst of speed from his nine-year-old rival. Fourteen point six three seconds for the non-stick frying pan. That's got to be close to a world record if she can get it on the shelf without dropping it.'

Sharon, my sister, rolled her eyes.

He was still at it two hours later when we were cleaning our teeth.

'It's Sharon, Sharon's holding on to her lead around the back teeth, but wait, she's slipped, her brush has slipped, oh no, this is a tragedy for the plucky youngster, she's missed a molar and Brendan has taken the lead, he's streaking home along the front ones, it's gold, it's gold, it's gold for Australia!'

Before we could remind Dad that shouting before bed gives kids nightmares, he herded us out into the backyard.

Sitting under the clothes hoist were three banana crates, the middle one taller than the others.

'The winners' podium,' announced Dad.

We stared, mouths open.

Dad had always been mad about sport, but he'd never gone this far.

Weak with shock, we allowed ourselves to be led up on to the podium, where Sharon received the silver medal for teeth cleaning and I was awarded the gold for not dropping the frying pan.

Mum stuck her head out the back door.

'Bedtime, you kids,' she said. 'It's eight-fifteen.'

'Crossing now to the back door,' shouted Dad, 'to witness a true champion in action.'

Before she knew it, Mum was on the podium having an old beer bottle top on a ribbon hung round her neck for telling the right time.

Over the next days, gold medals were won at our place for potato peeling, TV watching, ironing, getting up in the morning, pet care, closing the fridge door, vacuuming, chess, whistling, putting socks on, toast scraping, yawning, homework, head scratching, microwave operation, hiccups, sleeping, nose picking, sitting down, standing up, walking, standing still, begging a parent to stop, and chucking a plastic strainer at a parent.

'Love,' Mum said to Dad as he was hanging another bottle top round her neck (spin dryer repairs), 'don't you think you're taking this a bit far?'

'Over to the spoilsports' stadium,' said Dad, 'where it looks like another gold for Australia!'

As the days turned into weeks, we all wanted to scream.

Finally Mum did. 'That's it!' she yelled. 'If I hear another mention of medals, Olympics or personal best time in the loo, I'll kill someone!'

Dad muttered something under his breath about gold, gold, gold for getting cranky, then did what he always did when Mum blew her stack.

Took us to visit Uncle Wal.

Uncle Wal lives three hours away on a sheep farm.

It's a really boring trip because the land's flat and scrubby, the road's dead straight and you hardly ever see another car. Plus, when you get there, Uncle Wal hasn't even got a telly.

But this trip wasn't boring.

Half-an-hour up the track we ran out of petrol.

'It's a gold for Australia,' said Sharon, 'for forgetting to fill the car up.'

Dad glared at her.

We waited for an hour.

No cars.

Finally, Dad got sick of giving us medals for waiting and set off on foot back to the petrol station in town.

For the next hour me and Sharon just enjoyed the silence.

Then I started to wish I had something to read.

I read the car manual, the soft drink cans on the floor, and all the print on the dashboard, including the numbers.

Which is where I saw something very interesting.

I showed Sharon.

Then we saw a cloud of dust heading towards us.

It was Mrs Garwick from school in her van.

Soon we were speeding back to town.

After a bit I saw Dad in the distance, trudging along.

Mrs Garwick, who wears really thick glasses, hadn't seen him.

I distracted her attention by pretending to be sick in the back of the van.

She turned round, alarmed, and we sped past Dad.

Three hours later Dad staggered into town, hot, dusty and exhausted.

His shoulders drooped and he blinked painfully when he saw us sitting on the swings under a tree in the Memorial Park.

'Gold, gold, gold for Australia!' we yelled.

'Why didn't you stop for me?' croaked Dad.

Me and Sharon gave each other a puzzled frown.

'We thought you wanted to complete the distance on foot,' I said.

'Complete the distance!' shrieked Dad. 'It's forty kilometres.'

'Forty-two point nine,' I said, hanging a gold bottle top round his neck. 'Let's hear it for Dad, gold medal winner in the Olympic marathon!'

That was the last Olympic gold medal anyone in our family won.

We're all glued to the telly, though, watching the real gold medals being won in Atlanta.

All except Dad.

He's gone to stay with Uncle Wal.

Seeing Red
Alan Durant

Shanta, a young footballer, receives his marching orders after 'foul play'. He then has to play the same team in a cup match. What will he do when he is up against the player who got him sent off? Will he be able to control his temper or will he 'see red'?

You know that feeling you get when they're doing the FA Cup draw on the telly and you're waiting for the ball with your team's number to be picked out? That nervy mixture of butterflies-in-the-stomach and excitement? Well, that's the way it was at Grafton Park's training session that Tuesday evening when the coach, Bill Davies, called the team together to announce who they were going to play in the quarter finals of the District Cup.

'Right,' said Bill. 'I know you're all dying to know who your next cup opponents will be.' His statement was met by a breathless hubbub. 'What do you want first: the good news or the bad news?'

'The good news!' Jamie Lewis responded quickly with the authority of the team captain that he was.

'Yes, the good news,' agreed Shanta, the team's star player, and other voices supported him.

'OK,' said Bill, a smile on his round, healthily ruddy face. 'We'll be playing at home.'

'Yes!' cheered the team as one.

'And the bad news . . . ' Bill's smile became a grimace. 'We've been drawn against Barton.'

The response this time was more varied. Some groaned, some shrugged and one, Shanta, stood completely silent and still. When Jamie Lewis, who was standing next to him, turned towards his friend, Shanta's face was grim. It was as if he'd just heard that someone had died or something, not a cup draw.

'It'll be OK, Shanta,' Jamie said quietly. He put his hand on Shanta's shoulder. But Shanta shrugged it away.

'Barton,' he muttered glumly. 'Why of all teams did it have to be Barton?' He kicked up **a divot of turf** from the ground. Then, without another word, he turned and walked away.

It has been an excellent season so far for Grafton. They were currently top of their league, having won all but three of their matches, two of which had been drawn. Their only defeat had come at home and the team that had inflicted it upon them was Barton Green. The score had been 2–0, but the result told only half the story. For Shanta, the game had been a nightmare. Man marked throughout by a boy called Darren Powell, Shanta had hardly got a kick all match – well, a kick of the ball anyway; he'd had plenty of kicks on the legs and ankles, as well as jabs and shoves in the back, and all kinds of nasty threats and insults snarled in his ear. He'd come out of the game black and blue all over. But his tormentor had gone unpunished. Darren Powell was a thug but he was cunning too and had always committed his fouls on Shanta when the referee wasn't looking. A couple of times Shanta had complained, but the referee told him to get on with the game and stop moaning.

---

a divot of turf: a piece of turf

Finally, Shanta's temper had snapped. Reacting to a particularly painful dig in the ribs, Shanta had lashed out with his arm and caught Darren Powell full in the face with his elbow. Darren Powell had fallen to the ground as if shot. When Shanta turned, he saw his tormentor writhing on the ground with his hands over his face – and they were covered in blood. It had looked worse than it really was – Darren Powell just had a bleeding nose – but unfortunately for Shanta, on this occasion the referee *had* been looking. Without hesitation, he had reached into his pocket and shown Shanta the red card.

'Go on,' he'd said sternly. 'I've had enough of you. Get off.'

Shanta had raised his hands to protest, but, well, what could he say? Miserably, he'd trudged off the pitch and back to the changing rooms.

The score at the time had been nil all. But with almost all of the second half to go, Barton made their extra man count, netting two goals late in the game to win the match and deepen Shanta's misery. Most of his team-mates had witnessed Darren Powell's vicious tactics and after the match they were very sympathetic. No one blamed him for the loss. But Shanta blamed himself. He was angry and ashamed and very unhappy. He was in tears all the way home. Worse was to follow, though. Following the referee's report, the league organisers had charged Shanta with violent conduct and banned him for the rest of the season. Shanta was devastated, but Bill Davies had sent a letter appealing against the decision, and a number of spectators who had been at the match had supported him. The ban had been changed to three matches, but with a warning that if Shanta were sent off again, he would be banned from playing in the league for ever. Now Grafton had drawn Barton Green in the cup quarter finals, and, in the first game back after suspension, Shanta would have to face Darren Powell. No wonder he was feeling glum!

The evening after Bill Davies announced the draw, the Grafton Park coach turned up unexpectedly at Shanta's house.

'Sorry to disturb you, Mrs Nawaz,' he said with an apologetic smile. 'I just needed to have a little chat with Shanta about the match on Saturday. I expect he's told you we're playing Barton.'

Mrs Nawaz beckoned Bill Davies in. 'He's not said a word,' she said. 'He's been quiet as the grave since he got home last night. Now I know why.' She shook her head knowingly, then called upstairs to Shanta to come down.

'I'll leave you two to it,' she said when her son appeared, frowning, at the top of the stairs.

'Thanks,' said Bill. 'We won't be long.'

Shanta sat opposite his coach with a forlorn expression on his face.

'Cheer up,' Bill chided. 'You've got a cup quarter final on Saturday to look forward to.'

'Yes,' Shanta mumbled. 'Against Barton. And Darren Powell.'

'So?' the coach persisted. 'Barton are nothing special and Darren Powell's just a thug.'

'I know,' Shanta grumbled. 'I've still got a couple of bruises from last time we played.'

'You're not worried about a couple of bruises, are you?' said Bill lightly.

'No,' said Shanta.

'What is the matter, then?' asked Bill. 'Are you scared of Darren Powell? Is that it?'

Shanta snorted. 'Of course I'm not scared of him,' he rasped angrily. 'I'd stand up to that creep any day. I'd . . . ' He cut himself short, glancing guiltily at his raised fist.

'That's what I was afraid of,' sighed Bill. He looked at the boy with unusual severity. 'If you can't control your temper, Shanta, then I can't risk playing you. This match means too much to the team. I know what an important player you are – heaven knows we've missed you these last few games – but I think I'm going to have to leave you out of this one – for your own good and the team's.'

'No,' cried Shanta. 'You can't do that.'

'I can and I will,' said Bill firmly. His gaze softened a little. 'Look, Shanta, you're a very talented lad. You don't want to ruin your whole football career before it gets started for the sake of one football match – even if it is a quarter final. There'll be other quarter finals – and semi-finals, and finals too, hopefully. Why not give this one a miss?'

He looked searchingly at his young striker. It would be so easy to agree, thought Shanta – to drop out of this one; the team would still have a good chance of winning without him. And if they didn't, no one would blame him, would they? *Oh, yes they would*, a voice in his head replied. *You would blame yourself*.

Shanta looked down at the floor. 'I want to play,' he said softly. Then, lifting his head so that he was staring straight into the coach's keen blue eyes, he added beseechingly, 'Please.'

For several moments, the room was tensely silent, while Bill Davies contemplated the dilemma that faced him. Then, at last, his features relaxed into a half smile and he nodded. 'OK, you're in. But,' he warned, 'one hint of trouble and I'm taking you off. Understood?'

'I won't make any trouble,' Shanta promised. Then he smiled for the first time that day. 'Well, except for the Barton defence. I'll give them plenty of trouble – trying to stop me scoring . . . '

'That's the spirit,' said Bill Davies happily. 'Let your skill do the talking, not your fists.'

'Barton Green won't know what's hit them,' said Shanta and his smile broadened into a grin.

A few days later, lining up for the kick-off with Barton Green and seeing Darren Powell waiting for him, Shanta didn't feel quite so confident. He felt unusually nervous: he was excited about the game, yet almost wished it was over. And it didn't take long for Darren Powell to make his mark. The match was only minutes old when the Barton defender gave Shanta a sharp tap on the ankle that made him hop up in pain – but out of the referee's view of course.

'That's for last time,' Darren Powell hissed. 'No one hits me and gets away with it. You're really going to get it now.'

He nudged Shanta in the back, pushing him forward. Shanta stumbled then turned with a glare at his marker. His face was hot with anger.

'I'm not scared of you,' he said fiercely. He would have said more too, only he suddenly remembered Bill Davies' words. Glancing across at the touchline Shanta could see the coach staring across at him and the heavy frown on his face. Quickly, he moved away. It was fortunate that he did, too, because at that moment Jamie Lewis threaded a pass through towards him. Shanta took it and, finding himself in space for once, with Darren Powell metres away, he was able to turn and run at the Barton defence. In a flash he was past two flat-footed defenders and in the Barton penalty box. As the goalkeeper advanced to narrow the angle, Shanta dummied to shoot, then rolled the ball sideways for Jamie Lewis to run on to and thump first time into the back of the net. Goal! Less than five minutes gone and Grafton were one-nil up! Shanta was delighted. As he ran back to the centre circle, he passed Darren Powell, who scowled at him unpleasantly.

'That's the last touch of the ball you'll get,' he snarled.

Shanta just grinned and said nothing. He didn't need to. Well, his feet had done his talking for him, hadn't they? He'd shown Darren Powell who was boss.

'Great run, Shanta,' Jamie Lewis congratulated him. 'Thanks for the pass. I thought you were going to shoot yourself.'

'Well, maybe I will next time,' said Shanta happily. He'd get another chance soon, he was sure of that.

But his confidence was misplaced. Darren Powell may not have been the most skilful footballer on the pitch, but he was a strong defender – and he was as good as his word: for the rest of the first half, Shanta hardly touched the ball. Every time a pass was hit in his direction, Darren Powell intercepted it or tackled Shanta before he had the chance to get the space to move away. And in between times, when the referee wasn't looking, he used his full range of dirty tricks to try to hurt and provoke Shanta. The names he called him were even nastier now and Shanta was finding it more and more difficult to control his temper. He was just a step away from lashing out.

It wasn't just Shanta personally who was struggling. After their glorious start, Grafton started to lose their way and allow Barton back in the game. A careless mistake in their defence let Barton's central striker, Carl Hewitt, race clear to shoot home the equaliser. Even worse, in his brave attempt to save the goal, Grafton's keeper, Danny Marsden, landed heavily and injured himself.

'I think he's dislocated his shoulder,' Bill Davies announced glumly, as Danny was led away in tears by one of the watching parents to be taken to hospital. 'He certainly won't be taking any further part in this match.'

Grafton had a substitute, Jermain Stewart, but he wasn't a goalkeeper, so Bill Davies had to reorganise the team. Shanta's fellow striker, Mark Bridges, the tallest player in the side, went in goal and Jermain took his place up front. It wasn't a happy arrangement. With Shanta shackled by Darren Powell and Grafton's midfield passing badly, Jermain was unable to get into the game at all – while at the back, Mark Bridges had a nightmare.

In the space of three minutes at the end of the first half, Mark had let in two goals. The first, a rocket of a shot from Barton's captain, Ben Smith, wasn't his fault, but the second definitely was. Carl Hewitt's soft header seemed to be bouncing harmlessly into the stand-in keeper's hands, but somehow, Mark Bridges let it slip through. To the horror of the watching Grafton players, the ball trickled over the line for a goal. At half-time Grafton were 3–1 down and staring defeat in the face.

Bill Davies was furious.

'Don't you want to get into the semi-final?' he stormed. 'You're throwing the game away.' Brusquely, he listed the many things the team was doing wrong. His most stinging remarks were saved for Shanta.

'It's no good just waiting for the ball to come to you, Shanta, and letting Darren Powell say "thank you very much" as he takes it off you,' said the coach severely. 'You've got to move about. Make space.'

'But how can I make space?' Shanta grumbled. 'Everywhere I go, Darren Powell follows. Look at my legs.' He rolled down the sock on his right leg to reveal a collection of bruises.

Bill Davies shook his head. 'If I had another substitute I'd take you off,' he said. 'But I don't.' He gave Shanta a searching look. 'But if you really haven't got the stomach to cope with a marker, then maybe you should swap with Mark and take his place in goal. Let's see how he gets on against Darren Powell.'

Mark Bridges' face lit up at this suggestion. After his error in the first-half, he had no wish to stay in goal. It was a tempting offer too, Shanta had to admit. He couldn't do worse than Mark had done and he'd be free of Darren Powell at last. But just at that instant, he caught a glimpse of the Barton boy, leering across at him triumphantly – and Shanta's anger rose. He couldn't let Darren Powell think he'd beaten him. He had to stay out on the field.

'I'll move about,' he said sharply. 'Darren Powell will have to run a marathon to stay with me.'

'Good,' said Bill Davies. 'Take him all over the field, test his stamina. And if you still can't shake him off, then come deeper, into your own half and let Jamie push on up front. I'll give you the sign. OK?'

'OK,' said Shanta. Then it was time to line up for the second-half.

As the Grafton players jogged to their positions, the coach put a hand on Shanta's arm. 'Remember, Shanta,' he said quietly, 'keep your anger in your feet. Hit Barton where it really hurts – in their goal.'

'I'll try,' Shanta promised. But trying wasn't enough, he knew: he had to succeed.

Grafton started the second half as they had the first, with some good, flowing attacks, going close to scoring on two occasions. Then, at last, they got their reward when Jamie Lewis tapped in his second goal following a corner. Shanta, however, still couldn't get into the game. He moved from wing to wing to try and find space, but he couldn't shake off his marker. All he got for his trouble were a couple more bruises. Darren Powell was starting to breathe quite heavily now, though, and no longer had the puff to utter his insults, which encouraged Shanta to carry on with his running.

'I've got you now,' he said to himself.

But Darren Powell was nothing if not determined. His breathing got more and more laboured yet he wouldn't let Shanta escape his clutches – and his off-the-ball tricks got more vicious. As Grafton attacked down their right side, Shanta moved to sprint towards the centre from the position he'd taken up out on the left wing. He'd barely taken two steps, though, when his legs were swept from under him and he collapsed to the ground.

'Ah!' he cried, clutching his left ankle, which had twisted in the fall.

'Had a nice trip?' sneered Darren Powell, standing over him. The Barton boy's taunting words and expression made Shanta see red. A jolt of anger surged through him.

'You dirty thug!' he hissed, lifting his foot to kick out . . . It was the sound of his coach's voice, calling from the nearby touch-line, that stopped him. Shanta dropped his leg and, gingerly, got up on his feet.

'Shanta!' Bill Davies called again. Glancing aside, Shanta saw his coach jerk a thumb in the direction of the Grafton half. Shanta nodded, then, limping slightly, he trotted away from his marker, who watched him with a look of hard satisfaction. This time, he didn't bother trying to follow.

There were barely ten minutes of the match left now. Grafton were trying hard, but their early second-half pressure had eased through tiredness. The Barton players were weary too but they kept on battling with everyone back behind the ball. Only something special, it seemed, could unlock their defence – and Shanta was the one to provide it. Taking the ball from Mark Bridges, deep in his own half, he sprinted forward. As a man, the Barton side fell back before him and he was able to get half-way into his opponents' half before someone came to challenge him. Shanta swerved past him and quickly eased by a second tackle too. There were still plenty of Barton players between him and the goal, though.

As Shanta looked up to see who was free in front of him, Jamie Lewis made a darting run across the penalty box towards him. Shanta shaped as if to pass to him, but held on to the ball instead, moving inside towards the Barton goal. Two Barton defenders had gone with Jamie Lewis, expecting him to get the ball and, now, suddenly, a gap had opened in the heart of the Barton defence. Shanta needed no second invitation. Quick as a flash, he was through the gap and bearing down on the Barton goal. Unsure whether to come or stay, the Barton keeper dithered and by the time he'd made up his mind to advance it was too late. Shanta had slipped the ball past him and into the corner of the net. Grafton had equalised! It was 3–3. Shanta slid to the ground in delight, as his team-mates ran to congratulate him.

'Great goal, son!' Bill Davies shouted from the touchline, his round face ruddier than ever. 'Now, let's have another one!'

Shanta did his best to oblige. In the next few minutes he got more good touches of the ball than he'd had in the whole game up till then. Twice he set up clear chances for his team-mates with clever runs and passes, but each time they failed to make them count. As if gathering confidence from their good fortune, Barton mounted one last attack and won a corner. As he trotted over to take the kick, Ben Smith waved his team-mates forward. The Grafton penalty area was a mass of Barton green and Grafton blue. Only the Barton goalkeeper remained in his own half of the field. The kick came over. Jermain Stewart got his head to the ball but only knocked it up in the air. Darren Powell leapt high and headed the ball back hopefully towards the Grafton goal – and there was Carl Hewitt unmarked, on the edge of the six-yard box! It seemed that he must score . . . But no! Bravely, Mark Bridges flung himself forward to smother the ball just as the striker was about to shoot.

'Brilliant save!' cried Jamie Lewis. While all eyes turned towards the Barton goalkeeper, Shanta made his move.

'Mark!' he shouted. 'Kick it!' Then he turned and ran upfield. Mark Bridges' kick was a good one. Making full use of his striker's skills, he thumped the ball well into the Barton half. Shanta was away. His first touch, though, took him a little to one side of the field and by the time he'd got the ball under control and got back on course, he was aware of a figure snapping at his heels. Somehow he knew at once, even without seeing him, who it was: Darren Powell. Shanta accelerated forward, making sure he didn't push the ball too far ahead of him. Darren Powell followed doggedly. He may have been tired but he wasn't going to let his quarry go free.

Shanta was in the penalty area now, the Barton keeper coming out to meet him. Darren Powell was at his shoulder. Should he shoot now, even though the angle was bad, and hope for the best, or . . . ? He stopped and swivelled with the ball. Darren Powell was completely fooled. He ran right past Shanta, who came back inside and advanced on the goal. A shimmy left, then right and the keeper was out of it, lying helplessly on the turf. The goat was at Shanta's mercy. He pulled back his foot to tap home the ball and whack! For the second time in the match his legs were swept from under him by Darren Powell. This time, though, the incident had happened in full view of the referee. Instantly, he blew his whistle and pointed to the penalty spot. Then, beckoning to Darren Powell with

one hand, he reached into his pocket with the other. Picking himself up, Shanta watched as Darren Powell was shown the red card and sent from the pitch.

'That'll teach him, dirty fouler,' Jermain muttered. 'He should have been off ages ago.'

Shanta said nothing. The job was not yet complete. Coolly, he picked up the ball and placed it on the penalty spot. Then he turned and took a few steps back. The Barton keeper swayed nervously on his line. The whistle blew. Shanta stood motionless for an instant, then trotted forward and thump! The ball was in the net. 4–3! Grafton had beaten Barton with the last kick of the quarter final! As his team-mates leapt and whooped for joy, Shanta looked across to the changing rooms, into which Darren Powell was about to disappear, and he raised a fist in the air. Returning his gaze to the pitch, all he could see was the rush of blue that swiftly enveloped him.

My 1998 World Cup Story
Glenn Hoddle

What was Glenn Hoddle thinking when David Beckham was sent off in the 1998 World Cup when England played Argentina? Read on and find out . . .

Just before the second half kicked off I went to the toilet and got a bottle of water. As I walked back down the tunnel I checked with John that we'd covered everything. I settled down to try to focus on the second half . . . but within seconds came the bizarre incident that was to transform the game. It involved Diego Simeone, the Argentinian captain, and, of course, our own David Beckham.

It happened right in front of us, but much more importantly, right in front of the referee. David got a whack from Simeone and went down. As he was lying on the ground I suddenly saw this foot – his foot – come out from nowhere. David's head was still down on the floor, and he hadn't even looked to see where Simeone was. He didn't even know he was there. If Simeone had walked just two yards away from David rather than stayed parallel with him, David's leg would have come out and kicked air. Of course Simeone made a meal of it, making it into something far worse than it was.

But that doesn't excuse David. He should never have done what he did. When I saw it happen I just thought, 'What are you doing?' I thought about how many times we had warned him against that kind of behaviour, about reacting when provoked. It had been an issue ever since Le Tournoi, when a totally unnecessary booking had robbed him of the chance to play against Brazil.

However, I wasn't expecting a red card; I was expecting a yellow at worst. But it was red, for violent conduct. My stomach turned over again. How ever mad I was with David, I was furious with the referee. First, he hadn't produced a card for the tackle on Michael in the first half which gave us the penalty, and now this.

But I wasn't going to change the referee's mind. Nobody was. I had to get a grip. I had to concentrate on what I could change, I knew I would have to address the balance of the team. We had to cover ourselves. I had to decide whether to make a substitution immediately, or whether to wait and see how the game panned out. I thought about bringing David Batty on straight away to play alongside Incey in midfield. I even thought about taking one of the strikers off. However, I still wanted to try to win the game, be it during the ninety minutes or with a golden goal, and you can't win a game without strikers.

All sorts of things were running through my mind, and at that moment David Beckham wasn't one of them. Someone did go and see David in the dressing room but it couldn't be me. I knew I would have to deal with that problem after the game. All I remember is David untucking his shirt, looking back at the referee and walking off, his eyes staring straight ahead towards the tunnel. He didn't – or couldn't – look at me or anybody. It was a sad sight.

Nutty Footy
Martin Chatterton

How should you celebrate scoring a match-winning goal? The 'Nutty Footy' guide takes you through different ways you might try celebrating.

The '**Slide**'. A very simple dance which involves almost no practice. After scoring, run anywhere on the pitch and hurl yourself feet first along the grass, arms stretched upwards. WARNING! Do not attempt this on an artificial pitch or anywhere near the goalposts.

The **'Groove'**. This routine can be seen whenever a young player with a floppy haircut scores. Face the crowd. Point both arms at the crowd. Carefully place your left hand on your right shoulder and your right hand on your left shoulder. Drop your bottom towards the floor and give it a wiggle. Unfold your arms and point at the crowd again before running off. WARNING! On no account attempt this if you are: bald, over the age of 21, prefer the music of Phil Collins or you are facing the opponent's fans. This is because this dance has a TURKEY FACTOR of 42!

The **'Fighter Pilot'**. Popular with players who do not normally score. Because of this they go completely batty when a goal does manage to scrape in. As you score, extend both arms straight out at right angles to the body. They should now look like 'wings'. Without stopping, turn sharply away from goal and run around your team mates, arms still outstretched IMITATING A FIGHTER PILOT! Yes, it's amazingly stupid. One small tip: Do not run too near your team as serious injury can result.

The **'Corner Flag Samba'**. First seen during the 1990 World Cup. On that occasion Roger Milla, the Cameroon striker, scored, sprinted to the corner flag and danced the Samba with it. This has since been copied around the world, although it doesn't have quite the same exotic flavour at a January mudbath in Cleckheaton.

The Step by Step Guide to After Goal Dancing.

Here's one for you to practise at home.

Step 1: Keep the left leg straight with toes pointing forward. Lift the right leg and complete a double aerial back loop.

Step 2: Lift the left leg over the right shoulder. AT THE SAME TIME, extend the right arm to full length and wave at the crowd.

Step 3: Place the left hand on the right ankle, grasp firmly. Place right hand on left ankle, grasp firmly.

Step 4: Thread both feet through mouth and out of ears.

Congratulations! You have completed your first Nutty Footy After Goal Dance!

Greatest Sports Champions
David Somerville

Magic Johnson is one of the all-time basketball greats. Read on and find out why . . .

Magic Johnson
USA, born 1959

Earvin 'Magic' Johnson was one of basketball's greatest stars. He joined the Los Angeles Lakers from the Michigan State Spartans in 1979 and soon showed the fans what he could do. In his first season in 1980, he played in the **NBA** finals. He scored an astonishing forty-two points, fifteen rebounds and seven assists. He walked off the court with the playoffs' most valued player (MVP) award.

Johnson was unusually tall for a **point guard** at 2.06 metres, but had great handling and passing skills. Throughout his career he played with the Lakers. They were the best team in the basketball league in the 1980s, winning the NBA

NBA: National Basketball Association
point guard: This player is the most active in the team, dribbling the ball up the court so that a team mate can shoot. Normally this player is one of the smallest and quickest.

title five times. They were finalists on three more occasions.

Magic Johnson was named as NBA MVP three times in 1987, 1989 and 1990. But shortly before the start of the 1991 NBA season, Magic Johnson announced that he was retiring from the game. He had been infected with HIV, the virus that leads to the disease AIDS. However, he played for the US 'Dream Team' in the 1992 Olympics and won gold. Since then he has worked in the campaign against AIDS.

Magic moves in to take a shot.

Denise Lewis

Date of birth: 27 August 1972
Place of birth: Birmingham
Height: 1.71 m (5ft 8in)
Athletics club: Birchfield Harriers,
                  Birmingham

Denise Lewis

Denise's Heptathlon Highpoints

1994   Gold medal at the
       Commonwealth Games in
       Victoria, Canada
1995   Fifth at the World
       Championships
1996   Bronze medal at Olympic Games in Atlanta
1997   Silver medal at World Championships
1998   Gold medal at European Championships
       Gold medal at Commonwealth Games in Kuala Lumpur
       Awarded MBE for services to sport
1999   Silver medal at World Championships

The Heptathlon

Denise takes part in one of the most demanding competitions in athletics. Competitors have to take part in seven events in two days.

Day One
100 metre hurdles
High Jump
Shot Putt
200 metres

Day Two
Long Jump
Javelin
800 metres

The heptathlon has been an Olympic event since 1984. Before then, women used to compete in the pentathlon. This was made up of five events.

Activities

Olympic Marathon

1   Look back at the story and answer the following
    questions. Remember to use full sentences in your
    answers.

    • In which country does this story take place?
    • What sort of pet does Brendan have?
    • What job does Brendan's father do for a living?
    • What does Sharon win for cleaning her teeth?
    • How does Brendan distract Mrs Garwick?
    • How far does Dad have to walk?
    • Why do you think Dad doesn't watch the
      Atlanta Olympics?

2   Dad keeps pretending to give out Olympic medals
    for anything anyone does. Usually he does this in
    direct speech (page 3):

    *'Over to the spoilsports' stadium,' said Dad, 'where
    it looks like another gold for Australia!'*

    On page 3 there is a list of other things for which Dad
    pretends to give gold medals. Imagine what Dad might
    actually have said, for instance:

    Dad gives a gold medal for potato peeling:

    And here we are in the spud-o-drome, where young
    Brendan is going well. Lovely action with the peeler,
    it could be a new Olympic record!

    • Choose four things from the list.
    • Write down what you think Dad might actually have
      said. Write in direct speech. Remember to use the
      correct punctuation!

3   Brendan and Sharon are embarrassed by their Dad's
         behaviour. Do you have any embarrassing friends
         or relatives?

   • Write a short description of a relative or friend
     who does something that makes your toes curl
     with embarrassment.
   • Write a letter to this person, explaining as kindly as
     possible why you find their behaviour embarrassing,
     and asking them to stop. (Use your own address and
     today's date.)

Seeing Red

1   A reporter made some notes on the first half of the match
    between Grafton Park and Barton Green. Read what they
    said.

> Grafton made a bright opening. First goal scored by
> Jamie Lewis. This followed a delightful move from
> Shanta (Grafton striker) . . . beat two defenders . . .
> sold the goalkeeper a dummy . . . rolled the ball to
> Lewis . . . Lewis scored.
>
>   Grafton started to struggle. Darren Powell
> (Barton defender) marked Shanta out of game.
> Barton equalised. Carl Hewitt scored. Danny Marsden
> (Grafton keeper) injured. Mark Bridges (Grafton
> striker) forced to play in goal. Barton scored two
> more goals before interval.

These notes are difficult to read because they are not
written in complete sentences, so they keep stopping and
starting instead of flowing smoothly.

• Write the story of the first half from these notes in
  6–8 sentences.

2   A keen Grafton follower has tried to report the second
    half in one long sentence! Help him to make it more
    interesting and enjoyable to read by writing his account
    out in **6–8 sentences**.

> In the second half, Grafton came out fighting and
> their second goal was scored by Jamie Lewis, then
> ten minutes from the end Shanta took the ball deep
> in his own half and rode two challenges and slipped
> the ball past the Barton keeper into the back of the
> net to level the scores, then the match was decided
> in the last minute when Shanta was again fouled in
> the penalty box and Barton defender Darren Powell
> was shown the red card and Shanta scored from the
> spot to make the final score 4–3 to Grafton.

My 1998 World Cup Story

1   The extract tells the story of when David Beckham got
    sent off. It is told from the England manager's point of
    view as he watched the match from the bench.

    Write out and complete the following account, which
    explains the same event as David Beckham might have
    seen it.

> The second half had only just begun when I was
> f_____ by S_____.
>   I was lying on the ground, and suddenly I k____
> h___. I hardly touched h___, but he f___ o___.
>   As soon as I'd done it I knew I was in trouble after
> what G____ H_____ had said following Le T_____
> when I'd been b_____.
>   When the ref came over I thought I w____ get a
> y_____ c___, but I never expected a red card.
>   I just pulled my shirt out and walked off. I didn't
> l___ at the M_____ or a_____. I felt s___.

2   From what Glenn Hoddle writes, do you think David
    Beckham deserved to be sent off, or was he the victim of
    a set-up?

    • Copy out the table below and write down two or
      three points for each side of the argument:

Villain	Victim
Beckham deserved to be sent off because:	Beckham was treated harshly because:

    • Discuss these points with a partner. Share your ideas
      with the rest of the class and take a vote to see which
      opinion is most popular.

Nutty Footy

1   Make a full-page copy of the box below. In it, draw
    pictures (or stick people!) and write instructions on
    another Crazy Goal celebration you have seen (or make
    up your own!)

Crazy Goal Celebration No. 34

TITLE: _____

\
\
\
\
\
\
\
\
_____

_____

_____

_____

_____

_____

---

2   Re-read the extract carefully and write down:

   • one word that means the same as 'run' (page 26)
   • one word that means the same as 'throw' (page 23)
   • one word that means the same as 'try' (page 23)
   • one word that means the same as 'push out' (page 25
     and page 27)
   • one word that means the same as 'pretending to be'
     (page 25).

Greatest Sports Champions

Look at the extracts again and answer the following
questions.

1 *Magic Johnson*

   • Which team did Magic Johnson play for before he
     joined the Los Angeles Lakers?
   • What position did he usually play?
   • What is an MVP award?
   • How many times did Magic Johnson play in the
     NBA finals?

2 *Denise Lewis*

   • What events make up the heptathlon?
   • What change was made in 1984?
   • What medal did Denise win in Atlanta?

3 Who is your sporting hero?

   Write a fact file on a sportsman or sportswoman you
   admire. Include the following information, and add as
   many details as you wish.

   • name
   • sport
   • nationality, teams or clubs
   • trophies, medals, awards, records etc
   • greatest performance(s)
   • what (in your opinion) makes this person special?

Comparing Texts

1   Design a website for your favourite sport. Use pictures
    cut from newspapers or magazines, or draw your own.
    You will need to design:

A home page

- Say here what your favourite sport is
- Show pictures of action from your favourite sport
- Explain what is so great about it and why you think it
  should appeal to large numbers of people.

A 'dream team' page

- Make a list of all the players you would have in your
  'dream team' to conquer the world in your chosen
  sport, with facts about the stars you have chosen
  (*see* Activity 3 in *Greatest Sports Champions* for ideas).

A 'coming up' page

- List the most interesting fixtures/events in the coming
  season (either real or imaginary!) with pictures, profiles
  of opponents etc.

A sports reports page

- Set out all the results and best moments from recent
  matches, races or events.

A story page

- Choose a real-life incident from your favourite sport
  (like the extract written by Glenn Hoddle on David
  Beckham) and write a story based around a similar
  situation (like Alan Durant's *Seeing Red* on pages
  6–19).

  Then, add any other pages you like. You can design
  your website on paper, or on a computer screen. If
  you need some ideas, visit some other sports web
  pages on the Internet before you start.

Taking Off!

2 Comparing different types of writing

Look at the table below and match up the different *types* of writing in this section with the best description from the list below.

Write down the title of each extract in the right-hand column. The first one has been done for you.

Description of types of writing

- A person writes about their own life and experiences, and uses the word 'I'.
- A made-up piece of writing. It has descriptions of people and places. It can also have direct speech.
- A collection of facts about a person.
- A person writes someone else's life.
- Using words and pictures to explain how to do something.

Type of writing	Description	Title
Autobiography	A person writes about their own life and experiences, and uses the word 'I'.	My 1998 World Cup Story
Instruction		
Information		
Biography		
Story		

Section 2
Crime

Seventeen Oranges
Bill Naughton

When a delivery boy is caught stealing, he needs to think of a way out – fast!

I used to be so fond of oranges that I could suck one after the other the whole day long – until that time the policeman gave me a scare at the dock gates when he caught me almost redhanded with seventeen hidden away in my various pockets, and he locked me up, and ever since then I've never looked at an orange – because that gave me my fill of them.

I was driving a little pony-and-cart for the Swift Delivery Company in those days, and lots of my pick-ups were at the docks, where I could put on a handy sample load and be back at the depot before the other **carters** had watered their mares.

Now I was not what you call a proper fiddler, and I did not make a practice of knocking things off just because they didn't belong to me, like some people do, but just the same, it was very rare I came off those docks without a bit of something to have a chew at during the day.

---

carters: workers who drove carts

Say they were unloading a banana boat; well, I used to draw my little cart alongside. There were often loose bunches that had dropped off the main stalks. And when the chance came I would either make a quick grab, or some friendly foot would shove them towards me. Then I used to duck them out of sight under my brat. The brat was an apron made from a Tate and Lyle sugar-bag, supposed to be a good protection against rain and rough wear, but mine was used mostly for concealment. And for the rest of that day I'd be munching away at bananas, even though I hadn't a passion for them like I had for oranges.

But mine was all done on the spur of the moment, more or less, and not worked out to a fine art, as in one instance with Clem Jones, who came out of the gates carrying a box.

'What have you got in there?' asked Pongo, who was the bobby on duty

'A cat,' said Clem, 'but don't ask me to open it, or the blighter will get away.'

'A cat?' said Pongo. 'Don't come it. Let's have it opened.'

Clem wouldn't at first, but when Pongo insisted he got mad, and he flung it open, and out leapt a ship's cat, which darted back along the docks with Clem after it, shouting. Two minutes later he came out with the same box, holding the lid down tight and scowling at the grinning Pongo, and all the way home he scowled, until in the privacy of his own kitchen he opened the box and took out a full-sized Dutch cheese.

I got caught because the string of my brat broke, and Pongo, after looking over my load, noticed my somewhat bulging pockets. He made me draw the pony-and-cart to one side, and then he took me in his cabin and went through my pockets. There were seventeen oranges in all, and he placed them carefully on the table.

'An example has to be made,' he said, 'of somebody or other – and I reckon you're the unlucky one. Now, my lad, what have you to say for yourself?'

I said nothing. I was dead frightened, but I forced myself to keep my mouth shut. I had read too many detective stories to make the mistake of blabbing. *Anything you say may be used in evidence against you*. I kept that firm in my mind, and I refused to be interrogated. Pongo, who did not care for my attitude, said, 'Righto, I'll go off and bring a colleague as a witness.' And with that he went, carefully locking the door behind him.

I felt awful then. It was the suspense. I looked at the walls, I looked at the door, and I looked at the seventeen oranges, and I looked at my brat with the broken string. I thought of how I would get sacked and get sentenced, and of what my mother would say and my father do.

There was no escape. I was there – and the evidence was there before me on the table – and Pongo had gone for his mate to be witness. I was ruined for life.

'Oh, my God,' I moaned in anguish, 'whatever shall I do?'

'Eat 'em!' spoke a voice in my head.

'Eh?' I asked. 'Eat 'em?'

'Yeh, that's right,' replied this inner voice – *'and then the evidence will be gone. But be quick about it.'*

I thought for half a second – then I snatched an orange, peeled it in a jiff, popped it in my mouth, crushed the juice out and swallowed it, swallowing the orange, and I was just about to squirt out the pips when the voice cried:

'*No!*'

'Eh?'

'*You have to swallow them too!*'

'What – the pips?'

'*Yes – peel an' all! Evidence.*'

'Oh – oh, of course,' and I forced the pips to the back of my mouth and took a handful of peel to help get them down my gullet.

'*Don't bother to chew,*' said the voice, '*it's a race against time.*'

It certainly was. After that first orange I took out my penknife and slashed the fruit into chunks and gulped them down as fast as I could pick them up.

I was all but full to the brim, with three oranges still to go, when I heard Pongo and his mate coming back. With a sigh I gave up, but the voice warned me to guzzle on, suggesting that the more I ate the less evidence there would be – and as luck would have it, Pongo and his mate were detained over checking-up on some outgoing wagons, and since the sigh seemed to have cleared up a sort of traffic-jam in my oesophagus, I set about finishing off those last few, and by the time the key turned in the lock I was consuming the final piece of the seventeen oranges.

'This is him,' began Pongo to his mate, 'I caught him with his pockets ramjam full of oranges – ' He looked to the table. 'Hi, where are they?'

'Whew,' sniffed his mate, 'I can smell 'em.'

I never spoke.

Pongo began to search. He looked high and low, went through my pockets, felt at my brat, but of course he found no trace of an orange. Finally he figured out what must have happened, but even then he couldn't believe it. *'Seventeen* oranges,' he kept murmuring – 'big 'uns at that! – how has he managed it?' But I said nothing. And he couldn't give me in charge, because he had no evidence upon which to commit me – and because I suppose he did not want to be laughed at. So all he could do was to **vituperate**, while I kept my lips shut tight, and then he had to let me go.

When I told Clem Jones about it he said that I had been very slow; he said that I could have sued Pongo for hundreds of pounds because of wrongful detention, if only I had been quick-witted enough. But I never was a vindictive sort, and anyway, it was days and days before I could stand really still and think things out, because those seventeen oranges – peel, pips, and all – kept working away in my inside something shocking.

---

vituperate: speak abusively

The Lost Diary of Shakespeare's Ghost Writer

Steve Barlow and Steve Skidmore

Eggbert Noah Bacon (Streaky to his friends) is the man who really wrote Shakespeare's plays (or so the writers would have us believe!). His diary tells us about the Gunpowder plot in a mixture of fact and fiction.

25th March, 1603

Roast my regalia! We're going to have a new King! People have been celebrating all night. There have been bonfires, dancing in the street and lots of wine and food was given away free; a lot of it by Catholics, who reckon that King James won't be as hard on them as Queen Elizabeth was. His mum, Mary Queen of Scots, was a Catholic and there's a rumour that his wife, Anne, is too! So after all the years of persecution, Catholics reckon they might be able to hold Mass* in church rather than in the cupboard under the stairs.

I met up with Will Shakespeare last night. He was celebrating with Ben Jonson and a tall man with a beard.

---

*A church service held by Catholics.

'Great news about James,' he laughed. 'Streaky, meet a good friend of ours. His name is Guy Fawkes.'

9th October, 1605

I gatecrashed a party at the Irish Boy tavern in the Strand. I went along with Will Shakespeare, Ben Jonson (who's just been let out of jail) and a few friends of theirs, including that tall man with a beard I'd met before; Guy Fawkes. I was introduced to them.

They were in a foul mood and I think I know why. Ever since the King wrote a pamphlet saying how terrible tobacco is, all cigar packets have had to carry a health warning.

I must admit, I agree with the King, I hate the filthy stuff, but cigar-face Shakespeare didn't see it like that.

HM GOVERNMENT WARNING
His Majesty King James says
Tobacco is very bad for you, the noo.

So watch out and put it out!

'First he gets at the Catholics, now this!' he wailed.
The others nodded.
'Something should be done about it!'
'Maybe something will, Will,' said Robert Catesby.
I wonder what he meant by that?

6th November, 1605

Galloping gunpowder! What is this country coming to?

Will Shakespeare went a funny colour when I showed him the paper. Perhaps he's relieved that the King wasn't killed. After all, we are The King's Men. What would happen to us if our patron ended up splattered all over London?

YE STAGE

6th November 1605   25 groats   Ye papere for ye luvvies

PLOT TO KILL KING

Yesterday evening a wicked plot to kill the King was foiled by the guards at Westminster Palace.

A man was arrested in a cellar full of gunpowder under the palace of Westminster. He gave his name as 'John Johnson', although this is believed to be an alias. He is helping the guards with their enquiries.

FIREWORKS

The King had been due to open parliament today. If the explosion had taken place, King James, Queen Anne, Prince Henry and many noble men and ladies would have died.

The King's chief minister, Henry Cecil, commented: 'It has pleased God to uncover the plot.'

In other words, he's being tortured

7th November, 1605

I was walking across London Bridge when I saw a crowd of people gathering round a poster.

As I read it, I went all goosepimply.

WANTED.

Powder Plot Plotters

The man taken on the evening of the fifth of November has admitted that his real name is Guido Fawkes

The following people are also wanted

Robert Catesby   John Wright
Robert Wintour   Thomas Wintour
Christopher Wright   Thomas Percy
Thomas Bates   Sir Everard Digby
Robert Keyes   Francis Tresham
Ambrose Rookwood

and anybody else who looks suspicious, people you don't like, old ladies with a squint, anyone who might be a Catholic etc etc.
Any Information to The King

I took the poster down and went to the Red Lion inn, where I found Will Shakespeare and Ben Jonson sitting in a corner looking worried.

I showed him the poster. 'Wouldn't it be a shame,' I said innocently, 'If the King got to hear that Mr Shakespeare, shareholder in the King's

own company of actors, is friends with Fawkes, Catesby, Rookwood, Everard and the rest of them?'

Shakespeare gave a nervous cough and looked at Jonson.

'I want a pay rise,' I said. 'A big one. *And* I don't want to write so many plays. *And* I get to ride on the horse when we go on tour.'

Without a moment's delay he said, 'Agreed.'

Isn't blackmail a wonderful thing!

10th November, 1605

The news on the street is that several of the plotters have been caught and are being taken to the Tower.

Some of them died while trying to fight their way to freedom. Given the choice between death and being in the Tower, I reckon the dead are the lucky ones. Dead lucky, you might say!

31st January, 1606

YE STAGE

31st January 1606　25 groats　*Ye papere for ye luvvies*

WHAT A SHOW!

The people of London were given a wonderful treat, as the Catholic traitors who had tried to blow up the King and Parliament were sent to their doom.

Yesterday, at St Paul's churchyard, four of the Westminster Eight (Sir Everard Digby, Robert Wintour, John Grant and Thomas Bates) received their marching orders. They were HUNG, then, whilst still alive, they were CUT OPEN and their INSIDES were taken out and BURNT. Finally they were cut into QUARTERS to make sure they wouldn't do it again.

Today the same fate is in store for Tom Wintour, Ambrose Rookwood, Robert Keyes and Guy Fawkes at Westminster.

Be there early if you want a seat!

MAD MEG'S ASTROLOGY:
I see a bad time for Catholics over the next few years.

Guy Fawkes
Leon Ashworth

The facts behind Guy Fawkes and the Gunpowder Plot.

DISCOVERY!

ON 4 NOVEMBER, the night air was cold and damp in the cellar beneath the House of Lords. Guy Fawkes shivered as he waited in the candlelight. All the gunpowder was in place. In just twelve hours, James I and his parliament would meet in the room above. Suddenly the candle flickered – the door opened. Seconds later, soldiers rushed in and seized him. Guy Fawkes did not fight back. With his hands tied, he was led away.

A MYSTERIOUS LETTER

Somebody had betrayed the plotters. On 26 October a letter had been delivered during the night to Lord Monteagle, a Catholic nobleman. The letter, unsigned, warned Monteagle to stay away from parliament on 5 November. It hinted at a 'terrible blow', but gave away nothing more.

THE PLOT IS UNCOVERED

Monteagle took the letter straight to Robert Cecil, the king's minister. He waited – and why, no one knows for certain – until 1 November before showing it to the king. The king had returned to London after a hunting holiday.

James took the letter seriously. His father had, after all, been killed in a gunpowder explosion. A search of Westminster was ordered at once, but strangely the soldiers found nothing.

The king told Cecil to order a second search. Around midnight on 4 November, the soldiers went back. In the cellar below the Lords' Chamber, they found 'a very tall and desperate fellow', Guy Fawkes, waiting calmly with the barrels of gunpowder.

CAPTURE AND DEATH

Sometime after midnight on 4 November 1605, Guy Fawkes was dragged into the king's chamber for questioning. He refused to give his name and was bundled away by soldiers to the Tower of London.

He remained defiant, refusing to name the other plotters.

After two days of questioning, all he confessed was that he might be a Catholic.

King James ordered that the strongest methods (torture) be used to force him to confess.

The Confession

A t last, Guy admitted that his name was Fawkes, not Johnson. Gasp by gasp, the torturers dragged from his lips the details of the plot. By this time, Guy Fawkes was a broken man, barely able to sign his confession.

The Plotters Meet Their Fate

C atesby and the other plotters had fled to the Midlands. Three days after Guy's arrest, they were hiding at Holbeach House in Worcestershire. Their gunpowder was wet from drenching rain and they foolishly tried to dry it before an open fire. There was an explosion which blinded John Grant.

Two hundred soldiers surrounded the house. With swords drawn, the desperate plotters met their fate. Catesby and Percy were shot dead by the same bullet. The Wright brothers were also killed. The rest were brought for trial to London, where Francis Tresham died.

THE TRIAL

The Gunpowder Plot trial was held in Westminster Hall. It lasted only hours. On 27 January 1606, Guy Fawkes and the seven other conspirators left alive were sentenced to a traitor's death – to be hanged, drawn and quartered.

The executions took place on 30 and 31 January. Soldiers lined the streets as Robert Wintour, Sir Everard Digby, John Grant and Thomas Bates were dragged on sledge-like wooden hurdles to the scaffold. Guy Fawkes, Tom Wintour, Ambrose Rookwood and Robert Keyes died the next day.

Guy Fawkes, the 'great devil of all', was last on to the scaffold. He was so weak that he had to be helped up the steps by the hangman but was strong enough to mutter a prayer. Unlike some of his friends, he died at once and so was spared further pain.

Why Commit Crime?
Alison Cooper

Why do people commit crime? Read about some different viewpoints.

What might make you commit a crime? If you were homeless, with no money, would you steal food? Or if you had a job in a bank and you had worked out a way of pocketing the takings without anyone finding out – would you do it?

Many people disagree about why people commit crime. There are probably as many answers as there are criminals. People's backgrounds and bank balances do not seem to play a part – anyone can be tempted:

- Wealthy business people can be driven to steal millions from their companies. Maybe they are simply greedy, or perhaps they feel great pressure to get rich quick.

- It is perhaps not surprising that people living on the streets are more likely to become involved in petty crime such as theft or begging.

- In rundown areas, people neglect their surroundings. Vandalism, burglary and street and car crime increase, and living conditions become worse as a result.

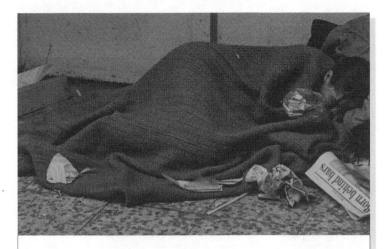

There are many other possible causes of crime.

> 'Unemployment, rundown cities, drug abuse, poor children and a widening gap between rich and poor create conditions that encourage crime.'

Safer communities, safer Britain, proposals for tougher action on crime

For many people, it is important to know the background and reasons for a crime before deciding what punishment is appropriate and how to tackle crime in the future. For others, the circumstances are of little importance.

> When John Major was Prime Minister he was not so interested in understanding crime. He just wanted to say that crime is wrong.

Those who share John Major's view point out that the vast majority of people living in poor social conditions do not break the law. Individuals decide to commit crime, they are not forced into it. But what about those whose behaviour is affected by psychological problems or mental illness? Child abusers, for example, have often been abused themselves as children. Is it right to understand such criminals 'a little less'? For some people, the answer would still be 'yes'.

> 'Many Americans are fed up with the idea of criminals as victims. They are against the argument that criminals with psychological problems are not responsible for their actions.'

US News and World Report

No one has yet found an answer to the question why different people commit crime. Some people think there are 'born criminals', who are more likely to commit crime. Some criminals might find breaking the law exciting or fun. Films might encourage violent crime by making it appear glamorous. If we don't know why people commit an offence, how can we choose a punishment?

Punishment and Law
Stewart Ross

Punishment today seems very fair compared to the horrible torture used on criminals in the past. This extract describes the terrible methods tried throughout history.

Medieval society was divided between peasants and a fairly small number of landowners and wealthy merchants. The rich were terrified of bandits because they were not afraid of authority. Rulers made laws that meant society worked in a way that kept them rich. Methods of trial were basic, and torture was widespread.

Horrific punishments, such as boiling and flaying alive (slicing off the skin), were designed to stop crime. But they could never put off those bandits who made a living by crime – or died of starvation.

Until the nineteenth century, the penalty for robbery remained death, though in the eighteenth century, a few lucky highwaymen were sentenced to repair roads instead.

Confess – Or Die!

Suspects were tortured to get information about other criminals, or to make them confess. Victims in extreme pain often confessed to crimes they had not done, just to stop the torture!

Tortures included gouging out eyes, and stretching on the rack, which slowly broke the arms and legs. Victims were also dropped into water. They were forced under until they confessed to their crimes.

Fingers and Toes

Hands and feet were a torturer's favourite target. Thumbscrews crushed fingers, so they could never be used again.

The 'boot' was a large metal shoe. The victim's foot was placed inside and the boot tightened with screws, grinding the foot to pulp. Many prisoners told their captors what they wanted to hear before the tightening began.

Cheap Punishment!

Today the most common punishment for serious crimes is to put people in prison.

But until the nineteenth century, prison was rarely used for the poor, because it was expensive. The authorities preferred cheaper punishments. The simplest were execution or cutting off a hand or foot. For less serious crimes, the pillory was often used.

The pillory had holes for the arms and head. Criminals were locked into these holes for a set time, and forced to stand in a public place where passers-by might throw stones and rotten food!

Mary Read, 1690–1720 and Anne Bonny, died 1720

Andrew Langley

Mary Read and Anne Bonny were two of the most feared pirates in the eighteenth century. Read about their adventures.

Mary Read's mother used to dress her in boys' clothes. When Read grew up, she liked to dress as a man, and worked first as an inn servant, then in the navy and then as a soldier in the army. After many adventures, she found herself on board a ship  which was captured by pirates. The pirates were led by Jack Rackham and a woman pirate, Anne Bonny.

Bonny also dressed in men's clothes and was the most feared fighter in the crew. She and Read quickly became close friends, and the leaders of the pirates. Together, they attacked treasure ships in the Caribbean. In one battle, the male pirates hid below in fright. Read shouted at them to come out and fight, and shot those who disobeyed her order.

Their adventure ended in 1720, when their ship was captured by the British navy. The men were hanged, but the women were spared because they were pregnant. Mary Read died of fever in prison, but no one knows what happened to Anne Bonny.

Activities

Seventeen Oranges

1   Look back at the story and answer the following questions.

- What is a brat?

    A brat is _____ (page 40)

- Find two words that mean 'throat'

    g_____ (page 42)

    oe_____ (page 42)

- Write down some verbs that you could use instead of 'eat'. You will find a few in the story.

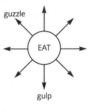

2   Find words and phrases that describe how the storyteller's feelings change during the story. Copy out the chart below and fill in these words and phrases.

Time	Feelings
When he was caught	
Just before he ate the oranges	
Whilst he was eating the oranges	
After he'd eaten the oranges	

3   As a class, discuss the following points:

- Do you like the character of the storyteller? How has Bill Naughton made you like him?
- Are you pleased that the storyteller got away with stealing the oranges? If so, why? If not, why not?
- Do you think the storyteller will steal again?
- How do you know that the story is set in the past? (Find clues in the story.)

The Lost Diary of Shakespeare's Ghost Writer

1   Re-read Streaky's diary entry for 7th November 1605. Now imagine that you are William Shakespeare. Write his diary entry for the same day.

> 7th November 1605
> I was sitting in the Red Lion Inn with Ben Jonson when Streaky came in. He was holding a poster. It said . . .

2   Write down the answers to the following questions. Remember to use full sentences in your answers.

- Why does Shakespeare agree to give Streaky a pay rise?
- What name did Guy Fawkes give to the guards when he was arrested?
- Where were the plotters executed?
- What was the name of King James's mother?

3   Write a 'Lost Diary' for another famous historical character. Do some research into the person and the period they lived in. Then use this information to write a few diary entries. Look back at the extract to see how to set out the diary. Remember you are writing as the person who is keeping the diary – you must use the word 'I'.

Some ideas for characters

- King Arthur's squire
- Henry VIII's jester
- Genghis Khan's hairdresser

Suggestions for opening sentences

- What a day I had today!
- You'll never guess what just happened!
- I knew it was all going to go wrong!

Guy Fawkes

1 Copy out and complete the following table.

Date	Event
26 October 1605	Someone writes a warning letter to Lord Monteagle.
	Guy Fawkes is captured
6 November 1605	
7 November 1605	
	The trial is held.
30/31 January 1606	

2 Imagine you are a government reporter covering the execution of Guy Fawkes. You can choose one of the following ways to present your report:

- as a newspaper article
- as a radio news report
- as a television news report.

Remember to include:

- what he did
- how the plotters were caught
- what happened to the plotters
- your opinion about the plot.

3 Imagine you are one of Guy Fawkes's friends. You think he was right to try and blow up the king. Write a letter to a friend, defending Guy Fawkes. It should be very different to the government report and should include:

- your thoughts about how Guy Fawkes was treated
- what you think about the person who wrote the letter to Lord Monteagle.
- what you think about the government
- what you should do next.

Why Commit Crime?

1 Below is a list of crimes that people commit. With a
   partner decide which crimes are the most serious and
   number them 1 to 7 (i.e. if you think murder is the worst,
   number it 1).

> **computer hacking**   **shoplifting**   **taking illegal drugs**
> **selling illegal drugs**   **speeding**   **joyriding**   **murder**

Think about your reasons for putting them in this order.
Discuss your reasons with the rest of the group.

2 Read the article again.

   • Write down three reasons why people might commit
     crime.
   • Do you sympathise with any of these reasons?

3 As a class, discuss the following points:

   • Why do you think people commit crime?
   • Do you know anyone personally who has ever
     committed a crime?
   • What happened?
   • Why did they do it?

Punishment and Law

1 The word 'punishment' is made out of a root word and a suffix.

Root word		*Suffix*	
↓		↓	
punish	+	ment	= punishment

'Punishments' has two suffixes.

Root word		*Suffix*		*Suffix*	
↓		↓		↓	
punish	+	ment	+	s	= punishments

- Which suffixes can you use from this list, to make more words from the root word 'punish'?

ing	ed	es	ly	ible	able	er	est	ful

- Make a list of these words.

2 **Word game**

How many different words can you make out of the letters used in the word 'punishment'?

Score: 1 point for every one-letter word
           2 points for every two-letter word
           3 points for every three-letter word etc.

Try and score more than 25 points! Who in the group can score the most?

Examples: in, ship

3 Some of the punishments described in this extract are pretty horrible! Is it right that we no longer use such methods to punish criminals? Or should people who commit wrong be severely punished?

- Organise a discussion or a debate with your class to explore this idea.

Mary Read and Anne Bonny

1   Use the library or the Internet to research some of the
    following topics.

    • Mary Read
    • Anne Bonny
    • Jack Rackham
    • Bluebeard
    • pirates
    • the Caribbean
    • the Spanish Main.

    Make some notes on the information you find.

2   Imagine you are a pirate. Use the information you have
    collected about pirates to write a realistic diary about
    your adventures.

    You could use the following entries to help you make a
    start.

    > 3rd July, 1719
    > Today we attacked a Spanish galleon. It was . . .
    >
    > 3rd August 1719
    > We landed at a harbour on . . .

3   Design a 'Wanted' poster for Anne Bonny and Mary
    Read.

    Remember to include:

    • what they have done
    • what they look like
    • how much the reward is.

Comparing Texts

1 Re-read *The Lost Diary of Shakespeare's Ghost Writer* (pages 44–51) and the extract on *Guy Fawkes* (pages 52–55).

The Lost Diary is a mixture of **non-fiction** (fact) and **fiction**. The *Guy Fawkes* extract is **non-fiction**.

- With a partner, compare the two extracts. Discuss how Steve Barlow and Steve Skidmore have mixed up fact and fiction in their retelling of the Gunpowder Plot story.
- Make a list of what is true and what has been made up. The list has been started for you.

Fact	Fiction
Guy Fawkes was a real person	Eggbert Noah Bacon is a made-up character
Guy Fawkes was tortured	There was no newspaper called 'Ye Stage'

2 In small groups, make up a drama improvisation based on a student getting caught shoplifting.

Practise the improvisation. When you are ready, present it to the rest of the group.

3 Imagine you are a lawyer. You have to defend one of the following characters:

- Guy Fawkes
- Mary Read
- the storyteller in *Seventeen Oranges*.

Write a speech saying why they should not be prosecuted. Re-read *Why Commit Crime?* (pages 56–58) to give you some ideas for your defence.

When you have finished your speech, read it out to the
rest of the group. Will they agree with you and let your
'client' go?

4   Copy out the table below, with the titles of all the
    extracts in this section along the top. Then look back at
    the extracts and match up the statements below with the
    titles by placing a tick in the relevant column (each title
    will have more than one tick).

State-ments	17 Oranges	Lost Diary	G. Fawkes	Punish-ment	Why Crime?	Read and Bonny
There is direct speech	✓	✓				
There are dates						
There are facts						
It is made-up						
There is no speech						

Section 3
War

The Lex Files
Robert Swindells

'Every boarding school has its ghost and ours is no exception'. Who is the ghost? Can Sophie and James solve the mystery?

I want to get one thing straight before we start. Me and James Otterbury aren't posh just because we're at boarding school, right? It's called The Cordwainers School and it's full of ordinary kids, including us. Me and James are a *little* bit famous now because of the skeleton, but before that, James held the school belching record and I could spit into a burger box from ten paces and that's all. Ordinary kids.

Every boarding school has its ghost and ours is no exception. Our ghost is a kid. It's known as the sad boy because everybody who's seen it says it looks really, really sad. Loads of people have seen it. The caretaker. The nurse. About a million kids, including me and James. No one's *spoken* to it though, except the two of us, and I don't think anybody'll get the chance now. If you're not doing anything special I'll tell you all about it, but I must warn you, it's weird. *Seriously* weird.

It's Thursday afternoon. D.T. with Ms Wheelwright. As we walk in she says, 'James Otterbury, fetch the spare workbench from the cellar. Go with him, Sophie Milburn.'

So, off we trot, the pair of us, along the dim corridor and down the old stone stairs. We're not thinking about ghosts at all because it's the middle of the afternoon and the sun's shining outside, but as we cross the cellar, James stops dead and says, 'Listen.'

I listen, and it's somebody crying. I don't know if you've ever heard crying where there's an echo, but I can tell you it sounds a lot sadder than ordinary crying.

I look at James. 'Who do you think it is?' Part of me's going, *the sad boy*. Another part says, *no way*.

'How the heck do I know?' whispers James. 'A first year I suppose, feeling homesick. It's coming from the far cellar, through the arch where nobody ever goes.'

The school's two hundred years old and teachers have been dumping stuff in that far cellar since the eighteenth century. You should see it. Anyway, it's coming from there and we creep in. The main cellar's got electric light, but if this one has, we can't find a switch.

James is right. It's a first year. He's sitting on an ancient stool, up to his knees in junk and with his head in his hands.

I was homesick in Year One and feel really sorry for him. I say, 'Missing your mum?'

He nods in his hands.

'What's your name?'

'Billings. Alexander Heracles Billings.'

'Good grief. All right if we call you Lex?'

Another nod.

'It gets better, Lex. Everybody's homesick at first. Anyway, it's the hols in three weeks.'

I'm looking at the kid's clothes. Something not quite right.

He sniffles, talks into his palms. 'Hols're no use to me. I'm stuck here. Forever.'

Then it hits me, of course. *The sad boy*. I look at James. 'It's – '

'I know, the sad boy.' He looks at the ghost. '*Why* are you stuck here?'

''Cause my bones're here.'

'Your b . . . *bones*?'

'Yes.'

'How come?'

And Alexander Heracles Billings takes his hands away from his face and tells us this story.

'It's 1940 and England's at war. There's bombing. The school's too close to the city so they decide to move it.'

'Move the school?'

'Not the building, you ass. The teachers. The children. To a big house in the country. It's forty miles away. Too far for my people to visit at weekends as they do here. I'm homesick as it is. I don't want to go, so when everybody's milling about with labels and parents and gas-masks and packets of sandwiches, I slip away. Creep down here. Hide. Oh, I don't expect to get away with it. Can't think of anything else to do, that's all. I expect them to come searching but they don't. There are voices for a while. The sound of engines, then quiet. I'll wait till dusk, then make my way home. They won't send me away, I tell myself. Not when they see how unhappy I am. But at dusk, I find somebody's shut and locked the big iron gate at the top of the steps. I call out. Yell at the top of my voice.

The echo scares me silly. I think they'll notice the other end. Notice I'm not there. That they've left me behind. Somebody will come.

  But nobody did, because two days later something horrible happened. The big house in the country – the new Cordwainers School – received a direct hit from a stray bomb. It was a big bomb, the sort they called a Satan, and it practically destroyed the house. Most of my friends – it was an all boys' school then – were killed, and everybody assumed I was among them. So . . . ' He shrugged. *'Here I stayed till starvation finished me. My friends – they're all with their mums and dads now, but I can't go to mine because – '*

  'Because what?' I murmured.

  'Because my bones aren't buried. They're over there, in the corner behind that great cabinet. I could show you if you like.'

And he did. And then he faded out, and me and James went and told Ms Wheelwright. She didn't believe a word. Marched us off to old Chocky's office. His real name's Mr Barr and he's the Head. Turned out he'd *heard* of Alexander Heracles Billings. School records.

  So off we all go to the cellar and me and James show Chocky what's behind the cabinet and that's that.

  Old Lex gets a decent burial and me and James get new nicknames. I'm Agent Skull, he's Agent Moulder. The kids talk about The Lex Files. I hope he knows what's they're on about, old Lex. I hope he's having a good laugh with his mum and dad in that place where the hols go on forever.

The Airman's Sixpence
Helen Dunmore

Billy and Ruby are evacuees who have to live with Mrs Penbury in the Second World War. But why does she treat Billy so badly and what happens when the children decide to run away?

She keeps me up with her every night. It's as if she doesn't want to be alone. Even though it's nearly eleven o'clock now, she's just put three more big logs onto the fire. My cocoa steams on the wonky tin tray. She keeps back enough milk for my cocoa every night, and even sugar. Two spoonfuls. She always saves her sugar ration for me. There are biscuits as well. She watches me eating and her face is hungry. It's no good trying to hide a biscuit for Billy. She sees every move I make.

'Drink up, dear. Don't you like your cocoa?'

'Mmmm, yeah. Course I do,' and I pick up the thick white mug.

'There's no need to say "yeah", Ruby. After all, we aren't Americans.'

'No, Mrs Penbury.'

'Auntie Pauline, dear! You silly girl.' And she laughs, a tinkly laugh that's a bit frightening because it doesn't seem to belong to her. Mrs Penbury is big, and she's as strong as any man. She does a man's job. She's always telling us that. Men have to be hard.

*

The wind whines round the farmhouse. It sounds as if it's fingering the walls, trying to get in to us. But I don't mind the wind. I strain my ears for what I think I can hear under it. Yes, there it is. A sound that's even thinner, even sadder than the wind. I glance quickly at her, and clatter my mug down on the tray to cover the sound. Has she heard? She's frowning, staring at her feet. What if she gets up, goes to the stairs, listens? What if she hears him? I'm sure it's Billy. He'll have had another of his bad dreams.

Billy's five. He never used to have bad dreams, till we came here. We were in London before, with Mum, then before that we were down in Devon, with Mrs Sands. She was lovely. But she couldn't take us back when the bombing started again, because her daughter, Elsie, had a new baby. Mum didn't want to send us away again, but she got a job in the factory at nights, and that meant she couldn't take us to the air-raid shelter if a raid started. I would've taken Billy. I'm old enough. But Mum wouldn't let me.

'No, Rube. With you and Billy safe in the country, at least I've got peace of mind. I know I'm doing right by you.'

It was all right in Devon with Mrs Sands. We missed Mum, of course we did. But not like this. Not with a pain that gets worse every morning when I wake up and know we've got another day here.

It *is* Billy. I know it is. He's crying again. He isn't properly awake yet, or he wouldn't make a sound. He's crying in his sleep. I shuffle my feet, crunch my biscuit, slurp the rest of my cocoa.

'I'm ever so tired, Auntie Pauline. I think I'd better get to bed.'

She stares at me. 'I've only just put those logs on the fire,' she says, 'Don't you want to sit up a bit longer?'

She always wants me to sit up. I don't think she wants to be on her own. She likes me to keep talking, it doesn't matter what I say. When it's quiet, she looks as if she's listening out for things I can't hear.

But I've got to get to Billy. I stand up, and put down my mug. I'm supposed to kiss her goodnight now. I've got to do it. She mustn't know that I don't like kissing her, or she'll be worse than ever to Billy. Her hair bristles against my face.

'G'night, Auntie Pauline.'

'Goodnight, Ruby. There's a good girl.'

There's a little oil lamp for me to carry up and undress by. Billy has to go up in the dark. She pretends it's because he's too young to remember about the blackout, and he might show a light. Billy is frightened of the dark. I go up the creaky stairs with my lamp flame shivering and bobbing on the walls. They are rough, uneven walls, because this is an old house, right on the edge of the village and well away from the other houses. It's a lonely house. Maybe that's why she wants me to sit up with her, even though at home Mum would've sent me to bed ages ago.

The whimpering sound is getting louder. I hurry. She mustn't hear it. I know what to do. I've got to wake him up really gently. I kneel down by his bed and put my arms softly round him. He's sitting up but I can tell he's still asleep. His eyes have that funny nightmare look in them. He is cold. I cuddle him close and whisper, 'Billy, it's all right. It's only me. It's Ruby.'

I keep on cuddling and whispering. Slowly his stiff body relaxes. I can feel him coming out of the dream and waking up. I press his face into my shoulder to hide the noise.

'It's OK, Billy, Ruby's here.'

He's shaking. Perhaps he's ill? But I look at his face by the oil lamp and I see he's crying. Fear pounces on me.

'Oh, Billy. You haven't. You haven't gone and done it again.'

And he nods his head, crying and shivering.

'Never mind. Don't cry. Ruby's here.' I hold him tight, tight. He's only five. My little brother, Billy.

'You look after Billy, Rube. You know how he gets his asthma.'

That's what Mum said when she was waving us off on the train, the second time we were evacuated. She thought it would be like Mrs Sands' again, and so did we. Billy was all excited, jumping up to look out of the window, waving at Mum. *'You look after Billy.'* Yes, I was right. He's wet himself. It's not his fault. It happens when he's asleep. He can't help it. But she mustn't find out. What can I do?

I can't do anything. She'll find out. She always does. And she'll put Billy in the cupboard under the stairs again, for hours and hours. It's dark in there. She says it's to teach him. *'He can't go on like this, Ruby. What'll your mum say when she gets him back, wetting the bed every night? She'll think I don't know what's right. Sometimes you've got to be cruel to be kind.'* He doesn't cry or scream when he's in the cupboard. I think she thinks he doesn't care. Oh, Billy. *'He's a boy, Ruby. No good bringing him up soft. You won't be doing him any favours.'*

Suddenly I make up my mind.

'Stand still, Billy, while I get your clothes. We're going home.'

I scrabble through the drawers. Clean pants, clean trousers, Billy's warmest jersey. His winter coat is on the hook downstairs. I'll get him dressed then we'll both get into bed and wait, wait . . . Once she's gone to bed, we'll go. We'll go home. Mum wouldn't want us to stay here. I know she wouldn't. She'll be working now, she works nights in the factory, but by the time we get to London it'll be morning. I don't care about the bombs.

When the last sound of Auntie Pauline going to bed has died away, we wait to give her time to go to sleep. I've blown out the lamp and it's dark. But I know my way round the house, even in the dark. I know all its lonely corners.

'Billy. Ssh. Hold my hand.'

The stairs don't creak. The kitchen doors opens and there's the smell of the slack she's put on the fire to bank it up for the night. Billy presses up behind me while I slide the big bolt back, very very slowly. It squeaks like a mouse. She hates mice. She's always leaving poison for them. The yard door swings open and black cold night air fills the space in the door-frame.

'Wait there, Billy. Don't move.'

I sweep my hand along the dresser. There it is. Her fat black purse with the big clasp. I weigh the heavy purse in my hand. My mum always said she could leave a penny out on the kitchen table all week.

'Ruby'd never touch it. Would you, Rube?'

'No, Mum!'

I was so proud of that. Mum let me go to her purse and get the shopping money out, because she knew

I'd never take a penny off her. Now I unsnap Auntie Pauline's big purse and feel inside. Two heavy half-crowns. A couple of joeys. A sixpence and a florin. I take them all and wrap my handkerchief round them. Is it enough to get us to London?

I hold Billy's hand tight as we shut the kitchen door behind us. The yard is full of shadows and we dodge through them to the gate. The lane is a tunnel of night.

'We can't go through the village,' I whisper to Billy. 'All the dogs'll bark at us. We'll go down the lane and across the fields.'

My chest hurts. Billy's too little, he can't run like I can. I hoist him up and carry him but he's too heavy for me and I can't carry him for long. He runs a bit, then I carry him, then he runs again. Each time I pick him up, he's heavier.

'You're a good runner, Billy!' I tell him, to keep him going.

The wind rustles the trees over our heads. There are sudden shapes and shadows. Something barks. Maybe a fox. We know about country things now. Then we come round the corner of the lane and a bit of moon shines on a big puddle. The road forks three ways.

'I got to put you down, Billy.'

He flops up against me. It's his asthma. Mum never ever lets him go out at night.

'All right, Billy, we'll have a rest.'

There's a stile and a path going across the fields. But no signposts. They've taken them all down in case the Germans come. Just the three lanes pointing off into the dark, and the path across the fields. Nowhere to say where the railway station is.

'You better now, Billy?'

He looks up and nods. I know he isn't, really. I stare round, trying to guess, trying to remember which direction the station is. We came from the station, off the London train. But it all looks different in the dark, strange and different.

'You wait here a minute while I look down the lane.'

But he grips me tight. 'Don't leave me, Rube!'

That's when I see it. A little red light that grows strong in the dark under the trees, then fades. Then it brightens again. I know at once what it is. My mum smokes and sometimes she comes in and sits on my bed in the dark and I watch the red tip of her cigarette winking at me. Someone's smoking, there under the trees. Someone I can't see. I grab hold of Billy. As we stare, a big shadow peels away from the trees and

moves into the lane. It's a man. A man smoking. A man in uniform.

I know all the uniforms. I peer through the dark and I see the shape of him. RAF. Straight away I feel a bit better. I like the RAF. He'll be on his way back to camp. Probably been to a dance. He throws away the cigarette and it skitters down the air and dies on the wet road. Then he walks slowly towards us as if he's been waiting for us, as if he knew we were going to come.

'Hello.'

I don't answer. But Billy pipes back, 'Hello' to him.

'You're out late,' said the airman. He's got a village voice, not a London voice like us. He must be from round here. I wonder where?

'Yeah,' I say. I look at him hard. Is it OK to ask him? I can see him quite well now because the clouds have blown back from the moon. But there's the shadow of his cap, too, hiding him. I clench my hand in my pocket, and it knocks against the money I've stolen. She'll be after me. She'll get me. They'll all believe her. *A thief. A little thief.* No one'll believe I had to do it because of Billy, except Mum. I've got to get to Mum.

'We've got to catch a train,' I say. 'My mum's ill.'

'Oh,' he says. 'The London train? The milk train?'

'Yeah. The milk train.'

Then I think, *How did he know it was London I wanted?* But I don't ask.

'It's this way,' he says, pointing across the fields. 'It's only a mile, across the fields.' Then he says, 'I'll go with you. Make sure you get there safe.'

Everything my mum's told me about strangers floods into my head.

'It's all right,' I say quickly. 'We can find it.'

'Over this field. Turn left at the stile and follow the hedge. Then there's a gate. Straight over and across that field and you come to the road. Turn right and it takes you all the way.'

'Is there a bull?' asks Billy in his growly voice. He thinks every field's got a bull in it.

'Couple of cows if you're lucky. Turn left, keep going, cross the gate, keep going, turn right at the road. You got that?'

'Yeah.'

'Mind you look after Billy.'

Did he say that or was it my mum's voice in my head? No, he did. *How did he know Billy's name?*

'You got money for the train?'

My hand closes over *her* hard, cold coins.

'I got money.'

He looks at me. 'You took it, didn't you? You don't want to go taking her money.' He digs his hand in his pocket and brings out a handful of notes and coins. He picks out two pound notes and a ten-shilling note and holds them out to me. But I step back.

'It's all right,' he says, 'You take it. I've no use for it now.'

So I do. I feel as if I've got to do what he says. Then he gives Billy a sixpence. 'Buy some sweets with it,' he says. Billy looks down at the sixpence and up at the airman. He doesn't smile or say thank you. Billy's always quiet when he's pleased. The man puts his hand on Billy's head, and rumples his hair as if he knows him.

'Give me that money of hers,' he says to me. 'I'll put it back for you. Then you're all straight.' I like the way he says it, as if he knows how I'm always all straight at home, with Mum. I'm not really a thief. I give him the handkerchief, and he unknots it and takes out the money. He puts it away carefully, in a separate pocket from his own money, then he looks at us again. This time the moon is full on his face. He is sort of smiling, but not quite, and under it he looks sad. He reminds me of someone. He looks like someone.

'Don't hold it against her,' he says. 'She can't help herself.'

I say nothing. He sounds as if he knows Auntie Pauline better than I ever could.

'Go on, then,' he says. I climb the stile, then he swings Billy up and over. I take Billy's hands and jump him down. 'I'll stand here,' says the airman, 'just to make sure you take the right turning.'

When we get to the other side of the field we look back and he's still there. He waves, pointing left, and I wave back to show I know what he means. Then we climb up the next stile, and over, and the hedge hides him. We go as fast as we can. There's no time to talk, but once we're safely on the road, Billy pants out in his growly whisper, 'He's still watching us.'

'How d'you know?'

'He just is.'

The wind blows round us, cold and sweet and smelling of cows and country things. We stop to catch our breath and listen. Ahead of us there's the shunting noise of a train and I know we're nearly there.

'Don't worry, you're not going back,' says Mum. She's been working all night. She's worn out and here we are on the doorstep and what's she going to do with us?

But it doesn't matter. Nothing matters now we're home. Billy's thinner and his chest sounds worse and when I tell Mum about the cupboard under the stairs she says she's going straight down the Evacuation Office to sort it out this very minute and we're not to move till she gets back. She goes off without even changing out of her overalls.

It's a long time before Mum comes back. Billy's asleep and I think I've been asleep, too. Things are all muddled up in my head. The airman, the dark lane, the feel of Auntie Pauline's money. How could he put it back? Mum flops into her chair and shuts her eyes.

'They're going to get on to her,' she says at last. 'Course, there's always another side to the story. Did she ever talk to you about her son, Ruby?'

'I didn't know she had a son. She didn't like boys.'

'He was in the Air Force. Died on a bombing raid last year. That's why she took you kids in, for the company. It must have been hard for her. Sent her a bit peculiar, I dare say, all on her own out there in the middle of nowhere, grieving for him. Not that it's any excuse, mind.'

'Don't be too hard on her. She can't help herself. Give me the money, I'll put it back.'

Mum sighs. 'I could murder a cup of tea,' she says.

'I'll make it,' I say quickly. I want something to do.

'Good girl. Seems she was so proud of him, being in the RAF. Oh, this war's got a lot to answer for. I suppose it got to her, other people's kids being all right when hers had gone.'

'But she was all right to me.'

'You're a girl, Rube. You wouldn't've reminded her of her son.'

I remember what Auntie Pauline was always saying: *'No good bringing a boy up soft. You're not doing him any favours.'* Was she thinking of her boy, and the war that was waiting for him when he grew up? I put the match to the gas and wait for the kettle to boil. I listen to the water begin to hiss in the bottom of the kettle. It's a sleepy, peaceful sound, and I shut my eyes.

Moonlight shines on the airman's face. He looks like someone I know. Who is it? The answer itches at the back of my mind but I can't quite reach it. He smiles. Then I know. It's Billy. The airman looks like Billy. So that was it. Mum was right, it was because Billy reminded Auntie Pauline of her own son that she was so hard on him. But perhaps she didn't mean to be . . . perhaps she thought she was doing the right thing . . .

The kettle changes its note and starts to sing. I open my eyes and look at Billy, sleeping on the kitchen settle. His face has a bit of colour in it again. His hand is shut tight, even though he's asleep, and in it there's the airman's sixpence.

Leaving Sarajevo
Judith Hemington

When Ahmed escapes from the war in Yugoslavia, he has to leave his own country to live in Britain. How will he cope with a new country and a new life?

Ahmed looked out of the window of the plane, and rows of ugly little houses in straight lines tilted first one way, then another, and queues of toy-sized cars seemed hardly to move at all.

The air hostess caught his eye. 'We'll be landing very soon. I'll see you out to the family you're staying with.' She spoke slowly, so Ahmed could understand what she said.

He nodded. He wanted to thank her, but he felt too miserable for that. If only he could just hide on the plane and then fly back to where he'd come from. He didn't want to be in England. He longed to be with his mother in Sarajevo, and for his elder brother and his father to be there too, and for everything to be as it was before the terrible war started.

For months and months when he had gone out in the streets he had run fast, his stomach tight with fear. But even so, he wanted to be back. He wanted to be waiting with his mother for his brother and his father to come home from the fighting that had swept them away.

When the letter arrived Mamma had cried and said how kind the people were to offer. She'd miss him so much, she said, but he must go.

'I don't want to go!' he had shouted.

'I want one of my sons to be safe,' Mamma said, and so he was here, almost in London, dreading meeting a family he didn't know. He still didn't quite understand why they had written. His mother said it was something to do with his grandfather – he wasn't sure what.

When the fighting began the English family had posted some food parcels, but only two had got through. The rest had been stolen. It was a shame about that, because there was hardly any food around in Sarajevo.

A few months had passed while papers were sorted out, and now here he was.

The plane shuddered and roared, and Ahmed felt sick with unhappiness.

There was a bewildering sea of faces behind the barrier. Ahmed blinked, and then caught sight of a cluster of people holding up his name in big letters. Without speaking he pointed the air hostess in the direction of the family, and she looked relieved, and hurried over.

Mr Feldman shook his hand. Mrs Feldman hugged him, but Ahmed held stiffly back. She wasn't his mother. There was a boy called Simon, who kept his eyes on his feet and said 'Hello' very quickly. He was about the same age as Ahmed, eleven or twelve, he thought. His sister was younger and was called Becky. She smiled in a friendly way and talked so fast Ahmed couldn't understand what she was saying.

They had a large, silver car – a Volvo – and Ahmed sank down in the back with Simon and Becky. Simon asked him what football club he supported, and Becky said: 'Oh no, don't talk about football, it's so boring!'

Ahmed didn't want to talk about anything. Sadly he stared out of the window. England seemed so different from Sarajevo.

'You're sharing a room with Simon,' Mrs Feldman said. 'I hope you don't mind.'

Ahmed had the feeling that Simon didn't particularly want to share with him. That made it worse.

'What would you like to do after supper?' Becky asked.

'Don't badger him. One thing at a time,' Mrs Feldman said. Ahmed didn't know what 'badger' meant.

'I expect you'd like to phone your mother to say you've got here safely.'

Ahmed's large brown eyes were full of gratitude as he turned to Mrs Feldman. 'Yes, yes – I would like that,' he said.

But the phone was in the kitchen, and the family were around. Mamma's voice sounded strange. He told her he wanted to come home, and she said he mustn't say that. He could feel tears coming into his eyes, so he couldn't carry on talking. He couldn't bear it if the family saw him crying. Mamma said she wanted to thank Mrs Feldman, so he handed the receiver to her, then rushed up to his room. He'd wasted the chance to talk, and now it was all over, and perhaps there wouldn't be another time.

For a while he sat on the bunk bed, breathing slowly, trying to force the unhappiness back down. After a time Simon's face appeared around the door. 'Supper's ready!' he said, and left before Ahmed had time to reply.

Ahmed tried to eat, but the food didn't taste like food at home. Each mouthful got stuck in his throat and refused to go down without several attempts at swallowing.

The family conversation around the table seemed to be happening far away. He could understand some things, but not all. His father was a musician and had travelled abroad with his orchestra. He could speak some English, and he had taught Ahmed. They could get some English programmes on the radio, too, and his family had listened to these. 'You must learn English!' his father was always saying. Ahmed picked things up quickly, but he found it much more difficult to understand what people were saying now he was in England. People talked so fast. It was too much effort to take it all in, so his mind wandered off. He kept picturing the day his father had to go away to fight, and his brother, and how empty the apartment seemed once they'd gone. There were some pictures that crept into his mind that were so terrible that he tried to push them away. There was the day a shell had landed near the bread shop. He had been standing so close to that spot only the day before. Everyone knew someone who had been killed and everyone was shocked and scared, and nobody went out unless they had to.

In Sarajevo he'd felt so hungry all the time, and now, there was food on the table and he had no appetite to eat.

After supper Mrs Feldman suggested Ahmed might like to go up with Simon to his room. Simon had pulled a face and, without speaking, had started walking towards the stairs. Ahmed wasn't sure whether he was expected to follow him, but he did.

'What d'you want to do?' Simon asked in a resentful voice.

Ahmed shrugged. What could he say?

'I'm watching TV,' Simon said, switching on the set in his room and fixing his eyes on the screen.

Ahmed wished Simon could be more friendly, but he was quite glad to have the television on. Although he couldn't really understand what was happening, except that the film was about policemen and crooks, at least with the television on he could just let everything flow over him. It wouldn't matter that he didn't understand.

That night when Simon switched the light off Ahmed lay stiffly in his bed and couldn't sleep. Simon was in the top bunk above him: Ahmed could hear him breathing, and he didn't want to toss and turn in case he was a nuisance.

The next day he stayed at home while Simon and Becky went to school. In the evening Simon's friend came, and he and Simon played games together, leaving Ahmed out. He didn't really want to be included, because he couldn't follow what they said to each other, but he wished they wouldn't make him feel so unwelcome. Becky was more friendly, but Ahmed didn't really want to be with her either.

'Simon will take you around at school, when you're not in lessons,' Mrs Feldman said on the day they decided he should go for the first time.

But it didn't work out quite like that. When they arrived at the school Ahmed was in a daze. He understood some of the things people said to him, but all the complicated instructions about where he should be, and when – all that was so difficult to follow. He was to attend classes with some other children who didn't speak English well, and a teacher told a boy called Michael to look after him.

'See you at break!' Simon said, but after he'd run off Ahmed realised that Simon hadn't told him where to meet. At the end of the two lessons Ahmed hoped the teacher would tell him where Simon would be, but he didn't, and Ahmed didn't like to ask.

'I see Simon now?' Ahmed said to Michael, who assumed that Ahmed knew what to do, and went off to be with his friends.

There were so many children streaming down staircases, hurrying along corridors, laughing and shouting. Ahmed felt panic rising inside him. Once he'd had a nightmare that he'd lost the rest of his family at the market in Sarajevo, and he felt as he felt then. Hopelessly he stepped out into the yard, threading his way through dense crowds. There was no chance of finding Simon in the crush of people. After a time he saw a teacher walking towards him, and he decided to ask her if she knew where Simon was.

'Sorry!' she said. 'Can't help. Try at the office,' and she pointed vaguely behind her, then rushed on.

Ahmed noticed a tall boy with very short fair hair and bulging eyes staring at him in an unfriendly way, so he moved quickly on, hoping he'd find the office without trouble. Behind him he heard footsteps. His neck tensed, and he walked faster. He didn't turn back to look. Then the footsteps behind him quickened their pace, and soon he found himself being nudged against the wall.

'Where you from?' the boy asked, putting his arm in front of Ahmed to prevent him from moving forward.

'I am from Sarajevo,' Ahmed said in a quick, quiet voice.

'What's that?' the boy asked.

Ahmed repeated what he'd said. He backed away from the boy, and a radiator pressed against his spine.

'We don't like foreigners here,' the boy said, his voice full of spite.

Ahmed was holding his breath, hoping for something to happen, something to allow him to escape.

A teacher came hurrying around a corner and, seeing him, the boy moved swiftly away. For a moment Ahmed remained where he was, trembling a little from the shock of what had happened. Then he wandered towards the office. Now he hated the school even more.

His eye strayed towards a glass door, and beyond that to tall gates, and a road. A loud buzzer sounded, and there was a stirring and scrambling to classes. Ahmed didn't know where he was meant to be next. It all seemed too complicated. Quietly he slipped out of the glass door, across the yard, and out of the gates. On the street the atmosphere seemed gentler and much less frantic than in the school. A little way down the road there was a bus stop. He joined a queue of people there, and before long a bus appeared.

A strange feeling had come over him. It was as if he were in a trance. He knew that he shouldn't be doing this – just travelling into the unknown, but he wanted to get away from that building with the unfriendly people and the conversations he didn't understand.

He gave the driver a coin. The man asked him a question. Ahmed nodded, and the man gave him a ticket. He wasn't sure where he would get off. Perhaps when most other people got off he would leave with them.

After a mile or so there were shops on either side, and the traffic was thicker. A number of people were edging out of their seats, so Ahmed rose and moved towards the door too. When the bus stopped, he got off, and then stood for a minute, bewildered, on the pavement. There were so many things in the shop windows. So different from Sarajevo.

His hand closed around the money in his pocket that Mrs Feldman had given him for his lunch. Already he was feeling hungry, but he decided he should wait before he bought anything to eat. As he walked along he avoided catching people's eyes. He thought they were looking at him strangely, but he didn't want to glance at them to check if this was just his imagination.

After he'd strolled around the shops for some time he caught sight of a McDonald's. He couldn't resist. He had to go in. Perhaps he wouldn't have enough money.

The girl who served him was friendly and helped him to sort out the coins for a Big Mac and French fries. They tasted delicious. Inside McDonald's he felt safe and comfortable, and so he stayed there for as long as he could.

When he came out it had started to drizzle, so he went into a large department store, and when that became boring, he slipped into another. Anxiety began to creep into his mind and spread throughout his body. What was he going to do? How was he to get back to the Feldmans' house? He didn't know where he was. It had been a stupid idea to leave the school. Where had he picked up the bus? Dusk was falling, and as the lights went on the place seemed different from when he'd arrived.

His mind was a blank. He stood still on the pavement, trying to force himself to think clearly. In front of him was a newspaper shop, and as he glanced at the stand outside the shop he saw a familiar name staring at him. Sarajevo. He looked more closely. There was a picture of bodies scattered over the ground. What had happened?

Panic began to take over. He needed to ring his mother . . . make sure she was all right. Wildly he looked around for a phone. He had to reach her. Soon. He couldn't bear not to know.

On the other side of the road he saw a kiosk, so he raced across and wrenched open the door. And then he realised that he probably hadn't enough money, and he didn't know how the phones worked.

Frantically his hand searched his pocket, and out came a little change. It was worth a try. Carefully he read the instructions, then lifted the receiver and dialled. The first time around he heard nothing. He tried again, and there was a ringing tone. All he needed was to hear his mother's voice. Just one word, to know she was safe.

No one answered. He waited and waited, then stumbled out of the phone box. Now what? He felt very much alone. On the corner of the street he saw a policeman chatting to a motorist. He remembered his mother telling him that British policemen were friendly. Could he ask him to help him to find the Feldmans' house? How would *he* know?

He decided against it but then, after he'd walked past, he changed his mind and came back. A pressing sense of urgency was building up inside him. He needed to get back to the Feldmans' to try to phone his house in Sarajevo.

The policeman listened carefully to what Ahmed said. 'Let me see if I can help you,' he said, and he spoke quickly into his radio. 'I see. Right.' Then he waited. After a while he spoke again. He glanced at Ahmed. 'I think it's the one. Yes. Yes. That's a bit of luck. If you send someone round . . . Corner of Beacon Street – near McDonald's. Right.

'Well, my lad, you've certainly got a lot of people very worried about you! If you come with me we'll take you back where you need to be.'

Ahmed bit his lip, anxious about having caused a lot of trouble, but relieved that he wasn't going to be lost in this unknown part of London for ever.

After a short while he saw a police car winding its way through the traffic. 'There it is!' the policeman said triumphantly. 'In you go, son. The driver can't hold the traffic up for long.'

As he sat in the back of the car his stomach turned over. Mr and Mrs Feldman would dislike him for this. They'd wish they hadn't arranged for him to come. Perhaps they'd send him back. Simon would be even more unfriendly. Then he remembered the picture in the newspaper of all those people lying on the ground in Sarajevo and he was sick with fear.

The car journey seemed to take a long time, but when the car stopped in front of the Feldmans' house Ahmed didn't want to get out.

A light appeared in the hall, the front door opened, and Mr and Mrs Feldman rushed down the drive. Ahmed hung back by the police car, his eyes on the ground. And then a wonderful thing happened. Mr and Mrs Feldman didn't yell at him or even speak to him in a stern voice. They both just hugged him tightly, as if he really mattered. Then Mrs Feldman said softly, 'Oh, Ahmed, you're safe! What a relief! We were so worried.'

'I'm sorry,' Ahmed whispered. 'So sorry I cause trouble.'

'Never mind. The important thing is you're back,' they said.

The Feldmans and Ahmed thanked the policemen, who drove off, and Ahmed followed Mr and Mrs Feldman into the house. Becky came rushing out of the kitchen, Simon behind her. 'Ahmed, I thought you'd got mugged or run over by a bus!' she said. 'What happened? Everyone was going crazy with worry.'

'All in good time,' Mrs Feldman said. 'I expect Ahmed just wants to settle down in the warm with some food.'

Ahmed gave her a grateful smile. All he could think of now, though, was of that newspaper picture. 'Please – I'm sorry I trouble you with one more, but could I phone Sarajevo, please? I saw in the newspaper a picture . . . ' He stopped, not sure how to explain.

'Oh yes, of course you'd be worried,' Mr Feldman said. 'It was on the news. You try phoning now.'

Ahmed felt his heart thumping inside him while he dialled. If there was no reply again, he didn't know what he was going to do. His fingers trembled as he picked out all the numbers.

He held his breath, and waited, and waited. Then suddenly there was his mother's voice at the other end. And joy came swilling into his head like an enormous wave.

He didn't stay on the phone long. He didn't need to, now he knew she was OK.

As he walked from the kitchen to the sitting room Simon came up behind him and tapped him on the shoulder. Ahmed turned round, surprised.

'I'm sorry I've been a bit mean since you came,' Simon whispered. 'I was fed up because Mum and Dad didn't ask me whether I minded sharing my room. It wasn't your fault, I know, but . . . I felt really bad when you ran off from school. I thought it was probably because of me – and if anything had happened to you it would have been my fault. When you turned up I was so glad! Shall we be friends now?'

Ahmed didn't understand every word that Simon had said, but he knew that he was being much more friendly now. He smiled at him, and shook the hand that Simon offered to him.

Then in the sitting room he drank a cup of cocoa and tried to explain to the Feldmans what had happened.

'Typical Simon not telling Ahmed where to meet him!' Becky said scornfully.

'No – not Simon, Perhaps I just not understand,' Ahmed said quickly, not wanting to get Simon into trouble.

'That's right – it isn't anybody's fault. It's that terrible war causing all the problems,' Mr Feldman said.

Later that evening, just before Ahmed was going to bed, Mr Feldman put his arm round his shoulder and steered him towards the sofa. 'Come and sit down here next to me – I want to tell you something,' he said.

Ahmed looked at him, wondering what he was going to say.

'My father came from Yugoslavia, as it was then – Zagreb,' Mr Feldman began.

'My grandfather came from Zagreb too,' Ahmed said, 'and then he comes to Sarajevo.'

'I know,' Mr Feldman said. 'And if it hadn't been for your grandfather, I wouldn't be here today. I expect you know about the Second World War.' Ahmed nodded. 'Well, my father's family were Jewish, and they were in a lot of danger when the Germans invaded that part, and your grandfather, who was a very brave man, hid my father's family, and he helped him escape from the country. Your grandfather and mine were both musicians, just as your father is. They played in the same orchestra. He risked his life for my father. My family have never forgotten that. So, as you can imagine, you're very welcome here, Ahmed. We owe a lot to your family!'

That night when Ahmed went to bed he thought about what Mr Feldman had said, and he was proud of his grandfather and much more at ease in the Feldmans' house. There was another thing to be happy about too. His mother's voice, telling him she was far away from the shell when it exploded. He'd feel homesick again, for sure, but at least he felt much better tonight than he had since he'd arrived. He knew he was welcome.

Ethel and Ernest

Raymond Briggs

This extract is from the moving story of Raymond Briggs' evacuation in the Second World War.

Farm Boy
Michael Morpurgo

Michael Morpurgo remembers what his father told him about *his* father's experiences in the First World War.

'Father was always getting into scrapes when he was a lad. But the worst scrape he ever got hisself into was the war, First World War. And just like with the swallow's eggs, he didn't want to fight anyone. It just happened. This time it was all on account of the horse. See, he didn't go off to the war because he wanted to fight for King and Country like lots of others did. It wasn't like that. He went because his horse went, because Joey went.

'Father was just a farm boy when the war broke out; fourteen, that's all. Like me, he didn't get a lot of schooling. He never reckoned much to schooling and that. He said you could learn most of what was worth knowing from keeping your eyes and ears peeled. Best way of learning, he always said, was doing. He was right enough there, I reckon. Anyway, that's by the by. He had this young colt, broke him to halter, broke him to ride, broke him to plough. Joey, he called him. He had four white socks on him, a white cross on his forehead, and he was bay. Turned out to be his best friend in all the world. They had an old mare, too. Zoey, she was called;

and the two of them ploughed like they'd been born to it, which they was, I suppose. Weren't a team of working horses in the parish to touch them. Joey was strong as an ox, and gentle as a lamb. Zoey had the brains, kept the furrow straight as an arrow. But it was Joey Father loved best. If ever he got sick, Father would bed down with him in his stable and never leave his side. He loved that horse like a brother, more maybe.

'Anyway, one day, a few months after the war started, Father goes off to market to sell some fat sheep. In them days of course, you had to drive them down the road to market. No lorries, nothing like that. So he was gone most of the day. Meanwhile the army's come to the village looking for good sturdy horses, and they're paying good money too. They needed all the horses they could get for the cavalry, for pulling the guns maybe, or the ammunition wagons, ambulances too. Most things was horse-drawn in them days. Father comes back from market, and sees Joey being taken away. It's too late to stop it. It was his own father that did it. He'd gone and sold Joey to the army for forty pounds. More like forty pieces of silver, I'd say.

'Father always said he was drunk and he didn't mean no harm by it, but I don't reckon that's any sort of excuse, do you? And do you know, I never heard Father say a harsh word about it after. He was like that. Kindest man that ever lived, my father. Big and gentle, just like Joey. But he had spirit all right.

'Couple of weeks later he's upped and gone, gone to join up, gone to find Joey. He had to tell the recruiting sergeant he was sixteen, but he wasn't of course. He was tall enough though, and his voice was broke. So off he goes to France. Gone for a soldier at fourteen.

'Now there's millions of men over there, millions of horses, too. Needle in a haystack you might think, and you'd be right. It took him three years of looking, but he never gave up. Just staying alive was the difficult bit. Hell on earth, he called it. Always waiting, waiting to go up to the front line, waiting in the trenches with the whizzbangs and shells bursting all around you, waiting for the whistle to send you out over the top and across No-Man's-Land, waiting for the bullet that had your name on it.

'He was wounded a couple of times in the leg, lucky wounds, he said. You were always a lot safer in hospital than in the trenches. But his ears started ringing with all the thunder of the shells, and he had that trouble all his life afterwards. He saw things out there in France, terrible things that don't bear thinking about, his friends blowed up, horses drowned dead in the mud before his very eyes. And all the while he never forgot Joey, never forgot what he'd come for.

'Then, at the first light one morning, he's on "stand-to" in the trenches waiting for the Germans to attack, and he looks through the mist and there's this horse wandering around, lost in No-Man's-Land. Course, Father never thinks twice. He loves horses, all horses, so he's got to fetch him in, hasn't he? Quick as a twick he's up over the top and running.

'Trouble is, there's a German chap doing just the very same thing. So the two of them met, right out there in the middle, both armies looking on. They tossed for it, honest they did. They tossed for the horse, and Father won. And ... you guessed it, when they got that horse back and cleaned him down, he had the four white socks, he had the white cross on his forehead, and he was bay. He was Joey. Takes some believing, I know. But it's true enough, I'm telling you.

'And that weren't the end of it, not by a long chalk. When the war was over, the army decided to sell off the old warhorses for meat. That's right, they were going to kill them. Kill the lot of them. They were going to kill Joey. After all he'd been through, all he'd done, they were going to have him slaughtered for meat. So Father did the only thing he could. He bought Joey back off the army with his own money, all the pay he'd saved up, and brought him home safe and sound at the end of the war.

'They had banners and bunting and flags up all over the village. Hatherleigh Silver Band too, just for him. I seen the photograph. Everyone was there, whole parish, shouting and cheering: "Welcome home Corporal! Welcome home Joey!" Always called him Corporal. Everyone did.'

Activities

The Lex Files

1   Lex tells the first part of his story (pages 73–74) in the *present tense*, even though he is telling Sophie and James about things that happened long ago. He only uses the *past tense* when he explains about the bomb hitting the new Cordwainers School, and what happened afterwards.

If Lex had told his story in the past tense, it would have begun like this:

> 'It was 1940 and England was at war. There was bombing. The school was too close to the city so they decided to move it.'
> 'Move the school?'
> 'Not the building, you ass. The teachers. The children. To a big house in the country. It was forty miles away.'

* Continue to copy out the story as it appears in the book, changing present tenses to past tenses, up to the sentence, 'Somebody will come' (page 74).
* Compare your version written in the past tense with the original written in the present tense. Why do you think the author chose to use the present tense for this part of the story?

2   The discovery of Lex's bones makes Sophie and James 'a *little* bit famous . . . '.

* Working in threes, take on the roles of James, Sophie and a radio interviewer.
* Improvise an interview for local radio in which Sophie and James each explain how they came to find Lex's bones. (Do you think they would tell the interviewer the whole story, or only those bits of it they thought would be believed?)

- Record your interviews on audio or video tape and play them for your class.

3 Answer the following questions, remembering to use full sentences in your answers.

- What record did James hold?
- Is the person who tells the story (narrates it) a boy or a girl? How can you tell?
- How old is The Cordwainers School?
- What was the name of the sad boy?
- What was the name of the bomb that struck Cordwainers School?
- What happened to the sad boy in the end?

The Airman's Sixpence

1   Read the story carefully and answer the following
    questions:

    • Why is Ruby dismayed that Mrs Penbury puts three
      big logs on the fire although it is nearly eleven
      o'clock at night (page 75)?
    • Why does Ruby shuffle her feet, crunch her biscuit
      and slurp the rest of her cocoa (page 76)?
    • Write down two things that Mrs Penbury does to
      Billy that make Ruby decide to take Billy away
      (pages 77–78).
    • Write down three things that the airman knows
      about Ruby and Billy that he should not have known
      (pages 82–84).
    • Who do you think the airman is? Give reasons for
      your answer.

2   **Character descriptions**

    • Draw or find a picture in a magazine, comic or
      newspaper, that could be each of the characters in
      the story: Ruby, Billy, Mrs Penbury, the airman and
      Mother.
    • Under each picture, write a short description of each
      character based on the information in the story. Use
      the character sketch of Ruby, below, as your model
      for the others.

> Ruby is kind because she looks after Billy. She
> is honest, because she never touched her
> Mum's money. But she is also determined
> because she decides to take Billy back to
> London and takes Mrs Penbury's money to
> make sure they can get home. She is sensible,
> because she tries to do what Mrs Penbury
> wants for Billy's sake, and she doesn't trust
> the airman at first . . .

Leaving Sarajevo

1 On page 97 Ahmed phones his mother in Sarajevo.
Judith Hemington leaves the reader to imagine what they
said to each other.

- Write out what you think they might have said in
  script form. The first few lines have been done for
  you.

  MOTHER: Hello? Hello? Who is it?
  AHMED: Mother? Mother? Is that you?
  MOTHER: Ahmed? Are you all right?
  AHMED: I heard about the bomb and I thought . . .

- Find a partner and read both your scripts out loud.

2 Have you ever thought of running away, as Ahmed does
in the story? Make a note of:

- what made you want to run away
- what happened (did you actually run away? If not,
  what stopped you?).

3 Research

Using the library and the Internet, find out:

- where Sarajevo is
- why there was fighting there which caused Ahmed to
  leave
- when this might have happened.

Old newspapers and yearbooks (1990–99) will also give
you information.

What is happening in Sarajevo now? Do you think
Ahmed would have gone back home, or do you think he
might still be in England? Use your research notes to
explain your answer.

Ethel and Ernest

1 Raymond is only five years old when he is evacuated, so his letter home (page 101) isn't very well written.

- Copy out Raymond's letter home, using the same words, but correct all Raymond's spelling and punctuation mistakes.
  (You don't need to correct the address and you can start the letter the same way: 'Dear Mum and Dad'.)

2 The last eight frames of the story on pages 100–101 show what happens when Raymond's parents hear that children are to be evacuated.

If this extract were told in *story form* instead of cartoon form, it might begin:

> *Ethel pointed a knitting needle at Ernest. 'They're not taking* **ours** *away,' she snapped.*
> *Ernest frowned. 'Course they are.'*
> *Ethel screwed her face up in anger. 'No, they're not!' she shouted. 'Over my dead body!'*

- Continue to write down what happens next in *story form* (to the bottom of the page), using direct speech as in the example above.
- Write down what Ernest and Ethel are doing and feeling as well as what they are saying.

Farm Boy

Imagine Michael Morpurgo's grandfather kept a diary. Here are four extracts he might have written. Copy out the extracts, then use your imagination to complete each one. Write what you think might have happened on each day, using the information in the story to help you. Include thoughts and feelings as well as actual events.

March 3rd 1915

I went to town today. I heard the army were recruiting for the war. I saw a sergeant. He asked me how old I was and I said sixteen . . .

May 15th 1915

In action for the first time today. I could hear the shelling getting louder as we got closer to the front. When we got to the trenches . . .

June 10th 1918

I still can't believe what happened today. It had just got light, and we were all on the alert because we'd been told to expect a German attack. I was peering through the mist when suddenly I saw this horse . . .

April 7th 1919

Me and Joey finally got home today. I thought I'd sneak into the village, quiet like, so as not to make a fuss. But as it turned out, the village had other ideas . . .

Comparing Texts

The most important characters who appear in the stories are:

> *The Lex Files*: Sophie, James, Ms Wheelwright, Lex
> *The Airman's Sixpence*: Ruby, Mrs Penbury, Billy,
> the airman
> *Leaving Sarajevo*: Ahmed, Mr and Mrs Feldman, Simon,
> Becky
> *Ethel and Ernest*: Ernest, Ethel, Raymond
> *Farm Boy*: Father, Father's father (who sells Joey)

1   Divide a page of lined paper into two columns, headed
    Characters I like and **Characters I don't like**.

   •   Decide which column each character belongs in and
       write their name in the appropriate column.
   •   For each character, give at least one reason for
       placing him or her in the column you have chosen.
       For example, if you like Ruby and don't like Mrs
       Penbury, you might write:

Characters I like	Characters I don't like
Ruby – because she is brave and looks after Billy	*Mrs Penbury* – because she makes Ruby sit up with her and she is cruel to Billy

2   Check your list with a partner. Do your lists agree?
    Discuss any differences of opinion.

3   Now write down a list of characters you feel sorry for.
    (You may find that some of these are characters you
    don't like.) For each character, say why you feel sorry for
    them.

4 The extracts in this section are all written from different people's points of view.

- First, complete the following table to identify the various points of view:

Title	Name of writer	Name of narrator
Farm boy	Michael Morpurgo	Michael Morpurgo
		Judith Hemington
The Airman's Sixpence		Ruby
	Robert Swindells	
Ethel and Ernest		

Now discuss with the rest of the class:

- Which texts are written in the first person? (I did, I said)
- Which texts are written in the third person? (he/she did, he/she said)
- How does this affect the way the story is told?

Do You Dare?

Moonies
Paul Jennings

Adam Hill can't read so he is tricked into signing a 'contract' by the school bully at his new school. Adam has to 'flash a moonie' at the School Principal. Will Adam go through with the dare and, if he does, will he be caught?

> *I, Adam Hill, agree to stand*
> *on the Wollaston Bridge at four*
> *o'clock and pull down my pants.*
> *I will then flash a moonie at*
> *Mr Bellow, the school principal.*

Who would be mad enough to sign such a thing? Suicide – flashing a bare bottom at Mr Bellow.

1

I'm going to explain what happened on the Wollaston Bridge. Then you will know the worst thing that has ever happened to me.

Normally I would never have agreed to sign the contract. Not in a million years. But I did. And do you know why? Well, I'll tell you, even though it's embarrassing. Even though it is something I'd rather not talk about.

The truth of the matter is: I couldn't read. I didn't know what I was signing.

I couldn't write. I couldn't spell. And I couldn't tell anyone.

Not being able to read was a big problem. I used to get into that much hot water over it.

Like, for example, when I ordered food in the hamburger shop. I would look up at the prices but didn't know what to order. Did it say, 'Hamburger with the lot'? Or did it say, 'No cheques accepted'?

Once I pointed at the sign and said, 'One of those, please, with sauce.'

The woman who was serving stared at me for quite a while. Then she said, 'You'll find the ladies toilet is a bit tough, love. Especially with sauce.' Everyone in the shop laughed. I ran out with tears in my eyes. It was no joke, I can tell you.

After that I worked out a new approach. I would listen to what the person in front of me asked for. If they said, 'One piece of grilled fish with chips,' I would say, 'Same again.'

Or they might ask for, 'A dollar of chips and two potato cakes.'

When it was my turn I would pipe up, 'Same again.'

That worked well because I always knew what I was going to get.

The only trouble was that I wasn't listening properly one day. I didn't hear what the guy in front of me ordered. 'Same again,' I said.

The girl handed me fifteen cheeseburgers. And I had to take them. It cost me a month's pocket money. I still can't look at a cheeseburger. You don't feel too good after eating fifteen of them.

Anyway, not being able to read and write was the pits. Especially when I started a new school.

'I'll write a note to the teachers,' said Dad. 'Then they'll give you special help with your reading. There's nothing wrong with that.'

'No,' I said. 'I don't want anyone at this school to know.'

Dad looked sad. 'Adam,' he said. 'You have to face up to it, not hide it. You're no good at reading but you can do other things. You're about the best drawer I've ever seen. Most people can't draw for nuts. Everybody's good at different things. You're good at painting and drawing.'

'Give me a week,' I said. 'Just one week at the new school before you tell them I can't read.'

He didn't want to do it. But in the end he agreed. My Dad is the greatest bloke out. The best. 'OK,' he said. 'But look, why don't you take one of your paintings? On the first day. Show them how good you are. Take that one of the wallaby.'

2

So there I was on the first day at the new school. Shaking at the knees.

Straight away I found out two things – one good and one bad.

I'll give you the bad first.

There was a bully at the school. Isn't there always? His name was Kevin Grunt but everyone just called him Grunt. He was big and tough and had a long nose.

It was almost as if he had been waiting for me. He took one look at me and then marched across the classroom. He whacked this piece of paper down on the desk. 'New kids have to prove themselves,' he said. 'Sign here. It's a contract.'

I went red in the face. Not because I didn't want to prove myself. No, not that. But because I didn't want anyone to know that I couldn't read. I had no idea what was written on that bit of paper.

I gave a little grin and held up my bandaged arm. 'Can't write,' I said.

I always used to put my left arm in a sling when there was going to be writing to do. That way no one would be able to know I couldn't spell. Easy. It never failed.

Except this time.

'Just write your name with your right hand, idiot,' said Grunt. 'Put a cross if you like.'

I looked at the piece of paper. Then I stared up at the faces that surrounded me. The whole class was waiting to see what I would do. I wanted to say, 'Will someone read it out, please?'

But of course I couldn't say that. They would all know my terrible secret. So I picked up the pen and scribbled my name with my right hand.

A kid with red hair and freckles pushed through to the front. 'I think it's mean,' he said. 'He's only a new kid. Give him a break, Grunt.'

'Shut up, Blue,' said Grunt. 'Unless you want to take his place.'

That's how I became friends with Blue.

'You're mad,' he said. 'You have to go out on Wollaston Bridge. At four o'clock. And flash your behind at Mr Bellow. There's nowhere for you to run or hide. You'll be in the middle of the bridge all alone. You'll get caught for sure.'

I smiled weakly. 'I could just go home,' I said.

Blue shook his head. 'Grunt and his mates will never leave you alone if you break your contract. Not now that you've signed. You have to do it.'

And the good thing? What was the good thing that happened?

Well, they were having this competition in Melbourne at the National Gallery. An exhibition. One person from each school could put in a piece of art.

Before the first period was over I found myself in Mr Bellow's office. He stood there looking at my painting of the wallaby. He shook his head. 'Fantastic,' he said. 'I can't believe that you are only thirteen. The Gallery director is coming tomorrow. I'm sure that she will pick this. It's terrific. We're very glad to have such a talent at our school.'

I was rapt. Maybe I would become famous. More than anything in the world I wanted to be a painter. I was never happier than when I had a brush in my hand.

I would have been the happiest person in the world – if I didn't have to go onto the Wollaston Bridge after school. And flash my bare behind at Mr Bellow.

To be honest, I am a shy person. I didn't want anyone to see my bottom. Oh, oh, oh. What a terrible thing. I just couldn't do it. But I couldn't not do it either. Could I? Not after I had signed a contract.

3

The whole school turned out to see the sight. Girls. Boys. Little kids. Big kids. The lot. They hid in the grass. Climbed trees. Every hiding place was taken. No one wanted to be seen by Mr Bellow.

So there I was. In the middle of the bridge. Kevin Grunt was clever. He had made sure that there was no hiding place for me. Mr Bellow would see my lonely bottom. Then he would see my face. And I would be dead meat.

Oh, the shame. Oh, the misery. The bushes were filled with giggling and laughing. What could I do? How could I get out of it? I didn't want anyone to see my behind. Bottoms are very personal things.

My knees were knocking. I felt like crying. I couldn't chicken out. Not with the whole school watching.

I looked along the road. A car was coming. It was Mr Bellow's Falcon. Oh no. Help. Please. Please. I can't do it.

I undid my belt. I fumbled with my top button.

The car was coming closer. My fingers were like jelly. I couldn't get my zip down.

Mr Bellow was so close that I could see his bushy eyebrows.

I pulled down my jeans. And my underpants. I was undone. My skinny backside was there for all to see.

With gritted teeth and closed eyes I turned and stuck my bare bottom up into the air.

There was a squeal of brakes. The car stopped. There was dead silence on the bridge. I dared not breathe. I tried to pull up my pants. But I was frozen with fear. I just stood there like a man before a firing squad.

Hopeless. Jeansless. Defenceless.

Mr Bellow stood there shaking. He was snorting through his nostrils like a horse. I have never seen anyone so angry in all my life.

He only said two words. But they were terrible words. They were words that spelled doom.

'Adam Hill,' he spat out.

Mr Bellow jumped back into the car and drove off. I knew that tomorrow would be the end of the world. Mr Bellow knew who I was. There was no doubt about that.

4

The funny thing is that the kids didn't laugh much. I pulled up my pants and started to walk off the bridge.

Blue rushed up and put his arm around me.

'Good on ya, Adam,' yelled out a girl with black hair.

'Good one, Hill,' someone else called out.

Quite a few kids came up and patted me on the back. They were all glad that it wasn't them who'd had to do it.

Kevin Grunt didn't like all this. Not one little bit.

'Pathetic,' was all he said. Then he and his mates headed off down the road.

I was glad that it was over.

Except that it wasn't all over. Not by a long way. In the morning I would have to go to the office for sure. Mr Bellow might kick me out of the school. What if he called the police? Baring your behind could even be against the law.

When all the kids had gone I took off my bandage and headed home.

'How did your first day go?' asked Dad.

I smiled weakly. I couldn't tell him what I had done. He would be so ashamed. 'Er, I think my painting of the wallaby is going to be shown in the National Gallery,' I said.

'Wonderful,' yelled Dad. 'Well done, Adam. I am so proud of you.'

That night I couldn't sleep. I just worried and worried. What if it got in the newspaper? What if the whole world found out what I had done? What was Mr Bellow going to do?

I tried to think of the worst punishment. Saturday morning detention. Expelled. Told off in front of the whole school. Mr Bellow complaining to Dad. The police brought into it.

But it was none of those. It was something worse.

I stood in Mr Bellow's office and stared at the carpet.

'This afternoon,' said Mr Bellow, 'the director of the National Gallery will be coming to see if we have a painting for the exhibition. We won't. We are not going to be represented by a boy who disgraces the school by revealing his private parts.'

He handed me back the painting of the wallaby.

My heart sank. Oh no. This was the very worst. I wanted everyone to see my painting. I wanted Dad to be proud. I wanted to be good at something. Before all the kids found out that I couldn't read.

I trudged back to class. Tears were running down my cheeks. I tried to wipe them off but I didn't have a tissue. I hoped that the kids wouldn't see I had been bawling.

5

When I got back to class there was no teacher there.

'The poor little wimp has been crying,' jeered Kevin Grunt.

I looked at him. I couldn't stand it any more. From somewhere deep inside I found a little speck of courage. 'You're a coward,' I yelled. 'You wouldn't have the guts to do what I did.'

Grunt looked around the class with a fierce expression.

'Yeah,' said Blue. 'You wouldn't do it.'

A few other kids joined in. 'Yeah,' they said. 'Let's see *you* flash a moonie, Grunt.'

'OK,' said Kevin Grunt. 'Just watch me.'

He grabbed a bit of paper and started to scribble on it. 'This is another contract,' he said. 'I'll flash a moonie myself. See if I don't.'

I looked at it. I could make out a few words but most of it was just scribble to me. I pulled out the first contract and compared them. This one looked just the same. But I couldn't be sure.

'We'll both sign it,' he said. He put his name on the bottom and held it out for me. I was in a spot. I couldn't very well ask him to read it out. But I had to do something.

'I have one extra requirement,' I said.

Everyone looked at me. I tried to think of something. Anything.

'I get to paint a picture on your behind first.'

A great howl of laughter went up. 'No way,' yelled Kevin Grunt.

'Chicken,' said Blue.

I thought that Grunt's face was going to fall off. He just couldn't take being called a chicken. He grabbed the paper and wrote an extra bit on the bottom. Then we both signed it. 'See ya after school, wimp,' said Grunt.

Just then the teacher came in and everyone scurried back to their seats.

At recess I told Blue that I couldn't read. He was good about it really. He didn't care at all and promised to keep my secret. He read the contract out to me.

'One word is different,' I said.

Blue nodded. 'It says Wollaston *Road* not Wollaston *Bridge*. He's going to hide in the bushes and stick his behind out. Then he will run off into the trees and Mr Bellow won't know who did it. He might even think it is you doing it again.'

'Oh no,' I groaned. 'I didn't think of that. I'll get the blame and Kevin Grunt will get off scot free.'

Blue was really glum. I could see that he thought I had been sucked in. 'And why did you say you wanted to paint his behind? What are you going to paint?'

'A wallaby,' I said. 'I'm good at wallabies.'

Blue looked at me as if I was crazy. 'If you paint a wallaby Mr Bellow will be sure it's your bum. He's already seen your painting.'

My heart sank. I sure was dumb. I was in trouble with Mr Bellow. Dad would find out for sure. And I had missed out on my chance to have my painting in the National Gallery. And now Mr Bellow would see Grunt's painted bottom and think I was flashing a moonie again.

I felt like screaming. But there was nothing I could do.

6

Everything happened just like I hoped it wouldn't.

There was Grunt. On Wollaston Road. He had picked out a nice little hole in some bushes. He was going to poke his bare behind out through it. Then he was going to run away unseen. And I was going to get the blame because one of my paintings would be there for Mr Bellow to see.

'Er, it's all right about the painting. I don't need to do it,' I said.

But Grunt was too smart for me. He had already figured out that I would get the blame. He even brought his own box of paints with him. 'Get on with it, Hill,' he said. 'It's in the contract.'

Well, all the kids were there. I had no choice.

Grunt dropped his daks and I started to paint away with my left hand. I couldn't think of what to do. 'Hurry up,' growled Kevin Grunt. 'He'll be here soon.' Grunt was having the time of his life. He knew that he'd tricked me again.

I had just finished putting the last dab of paint on when a car approached. Mr Bellow's Falcon.

We all ran and hid. Kevin Grunt stuck his behind out through the hole in the bushes. I closed my eyes and held my breath.

There was a squeal of brakes. A car door opened. Mr Bellow jumped out. So did someone else. There was a passenger in the car.

Grunt ran for it. He pulled up his daks and shot off into the scrub. There was no way that Mr Bellow would have seen who it was.

Mr Bellow stood there shaking. He was snorting through his nostrils like a horse. I have never seen anyone so angry in all my life.

He only said two words. But they were terrible words. They were words that spelled doom.

'Kevin Grunt,' he spat out.

Mr Bellow jumped back into the car and drove off. I knew that tomorrow would be the end of the world. For Kevin Grunt. Mr Bellow knew who he was. There was no doubt about that.

7

Well, Grunt really copped it. He was given three Saturday morning detentions. And no one was sorry. Not one single person.

Still and all, his punishment wasn't as bad as mine. I had missed out on having a painting in the National Gallery.

That night I was pretty miserable. Until the phone rang. 'For you,' said Dad.

'Yes?' I said into the phone.

I listened. I listened real good. It was the director of the National Gallery.

'I was travelling home with Mr Bellow today,' she said. 'And a painting stared out at me from the bushes. An unusual painting. I believe you were the artist. A left-hander they tell me.'

'Yes,' I mumbled.

'It was wonderful,' said the director. 'I want you to give us something to put in the Gallery.'

Well, talk about rapt. Dad was so proud. He went out and bought me a book about this painter Van Gogh who cut his own ear off. The words were hard to read. But it was so interesting that I started to get the hang of it. I just had to find out what happened in the end.

Blue was proud of me too. 'You're a genius, Adam,' he said. 'But you're lucky. How did Mr Bellow know that it was Grunt's bare bottom? And what did you paint on it anyway?'

Blue laughed when he heard my answer.

'I painted a face,' I said. 'One with a long nose. I think Mr Bellow recognised who it was straight away.'

Dare You
Robert Scott

'If you went in the graveyard late at night and lay down on a grave the ghost of the dead person would grab you and drag you under.' Jeanie takes up the challenge in this spooky tale with a twist.

They were sitting round trying to scare one another.

Jim told them about the creature in the Fens which his dad had seen moving about at night, but the others just laughed and said it was only Jim's dad trying to make him keep away.

Cathy told them about the woman who found a hairy toe and took it home to stew but the monster came after her and got it back. Jim and Kev had heard the story before and said that it was just a story.

Jeanie told them about the miller's boy who had been attacked one night by a huge black cat and had managed to cut off one of its paws before it vanished. The paw turned into a hand and the next day the miller found that his wife had one hand missing. She was burnt as a witch. Jeanie said that if you went to the old mill at midnight and said the right spell the witch would appear.

Kev said he didn't think there was any point in making a witch reappear, but if you went in the graveyard late at night and lay down on a grave the ghost of the dead person would grab you and drag you under.

'That's silly!' said Jeanie. 'What would it want to do that for?'

'I don't know, but it does, anyway.'

'Well, I don't believe it.'

'Huh! I bet *you* daren't do it.'

'I'm not afraid of anyone who's dead,' said Jeanie. 'They're just dead, that's all.'

Jim interrupted. 'It's not just anyone. It has to be a fresh grave. Someone who's just been buried.'

'You mean like old man Crosby?' Cathy asked. 'He was buried today.'

'Yeah,' said Kev. 'Dare you to go and lie down on old man Crosby's grave tonight.'

'Old man Crosby,' Jim said softly. 'He always was rather sweet on you, wasn't he?'

'He was a disgusting old man and I'm glad he's dead!'

'Yeah, but I bet you daren't go and lie down on his grave tonight,' said Jim.

'Dare you,' said Kev.

Jeanie was quiet.

'Go on,' Cathy said. 'You show them. You don't believe in ghosts anyway.'

'Well?' Jim looked at her, knowing his sister would back out.

'All right, I will then.'

'How will we know if she does it?' Kev asked.

'Well, you could all come with me, then you'd know.'

'Oh no we won't!' said Kev. 'You have to be alone. It doesn't work if you're not alone.'

'Sounds to me as if you're the one who's scared,' Cathy said.

Kev grinned at her. 'You bet!' he said. 'You wouldn't catch me anywhere near there tonight. Not with old man Crosby waiting to drag you down and spend the rest of eternity with him.'

'That's just plain stupid!' Jeanie shouted. 'Of course I'll go. We're not all as scared as you.'

Kevin winked at Jim behind Jeanie's back.

'I'll make sure she goes out after everyone's asleep,' Jim said.

'I don't need your help, thank you.'

'And you can borrow my knife,' said Kev, handing her his sheath knife. 'You can stick it in old man Crosby's grave tonight, then we'll know you got further than the gate.'

'You're not supposed to have that,' said Cathy.

'Oh, give over! She's not going to do it anyway.'

But Jeanie put the knife in her pocket and walked away.

Standing outside the churchyard gate at half past eleven that night, Jeanie wasn't feeling very confident. She shouldn't have let Kevin and her brother trick her into accepting a dare. She didn't believe in ghosts and she didn't believe in Kev's story about being pulled into a grave, but in that case what was she doing here? She didn't have to prove anything. She would have gone back but she knew that if she did they would keep on at her about being scared. She *wasn't* scared, but now she had to go through with the whole silly business.

And I bet the damn gate squeaks, she said to herself.

It did.

Jeanie shivered and pulled her coat tight round her. She could just make out the gravel path snaking between the shrubs and abandoned tombstones and followed it to where she knew old man Crosby's grave would be. She half expected Kev and her brother to jump out at her dressed in sheets, and she determined not to be startled. *Oh, hello*, she would say, *decided to come up for some fresh air, have you?* But they didn't appear.

Old man Crosby had been a vile old man: bad tempered, dirty, often drunk, he would sit on the bench outside the school watching the girls in the playground and shouting comments at them. From time to time he was moved on by the police or, less often, the headmistress, but he was soon back. He had been found dead in a shed on the allotments at the weekend and been hurriedly buried, unloved and unmourned, less than twelve hours before.

She found his grave, marked by a small bunch of ragged flowers, and peered round for any sign of the boys. There was none. Determined now to get everything over and done with as soon as possible, she took Kevin's sheath knife from her coat pocket and knelt down on old man Crosby's grave. She plunged it hard into the soil and started to move away.

She was caught. She tried to stand, but was pulled down again. She tried to roll to one side but was held. Terror gripped her. She moaned as she struggled again to escape, but couldn't. She remembered the time old man Crosby had caught hold of her when she crossed the allotments late one evening, and screamed. Nobody heard her.

Jim was at Kev's house before breakfast.

'She's not back,' he said, his voice shaking.

Kevin started to make a joke, but looked at Jim's face and thought better of it.

'What do your parents say?'

'They don't know yet. They think she's still in her room.'

'Are you sure she isn't?'

Jim looked at him. 'There's only one place she can be. Are you coming or,' he looked hard at Kevin, 'are you scared that old man Crosby'll get you?'

They found Jeanie's body sprawled across old man Crosby's grave. She was held there by Kevin's sheath knife, which she had driven deep into the ground through the bottom of her coat.

The History of Bungee Jumping
Steve Skidmore

Discover how the crazy sport of bungee jumping began.

Bungee jumping is one of the most daring sports in the world. Thousands of people have stood on cliffs, bridges, buildings and thrown themselves into space. They are stopped from falling to their death only by being tied to a cord or piece of elastic.

How Bungee began
People living on Pentecostal Island in the South Pacific tied jungle vines to their ankles. They then leapt from towers made from trees and branches. The jumpers attempted to get as close to the ground as possible without breaking their necks! They thought that this would help the harvest.

The first foreign jumper
Kal Muller, a photographer and author, was the first foreigner to take a jump. He visited the Island in 1970 and dived over 25 metres.

The first Bungee jump in the Western world
This was made by members of the Oxford University's Dangerous Sports Club. In 1979 they jumped from the 245-foot Clifton Bridge in Bristol, England. For the jump they dressed up in top hats and evening suits! They also jumped from the Golden Gate Bridge in San Francisco, America.

The longest Bungee jump
Gregory Riffi is in *The Guinness Book of Records* for his Bungee jump. In 1992 he jumped from a helicopter and fell over 610 metres!

Why do people do it?
Peer pressure and curiosity are the most common reasons people give for throwing themselves into space. However, the excitement can more than make up for the fear of doing it. The rush of adrenalin is incredible! A person's heart beat can go up to over 180 beats per minute as the jumper plunges earthwards at terminal velocity. As the elastic reaches its limit, the jumper stops falling and hurtles back up towards the place they have just jumped from!

A Bungee Jump

Internet advertisement for Shearwater Adventures and information on bungee jumping from Victoria Falls Bridge (one of the world's highest bungee jumps).

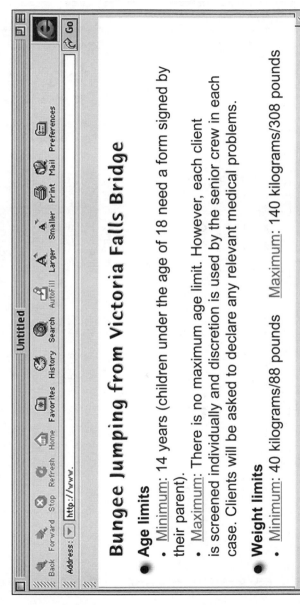

Bungee Jumping from Victoria Falls Bridge

● Age limits

- <u>Minimum</u>: 14 years (children under the age of 18 need a form signed by their parent).
- <u>Maximum</u>: There is no maximum age limit. However, each client is screened individually and discretion is used by the senior crew in each case. Clients will be asked to declare any relevant medical problems.

● Weight limits

- <u>Minimum</u>: 40 kilograms/88 pounds   <u>Maximum</u>: 140 kilograms/308 pounds

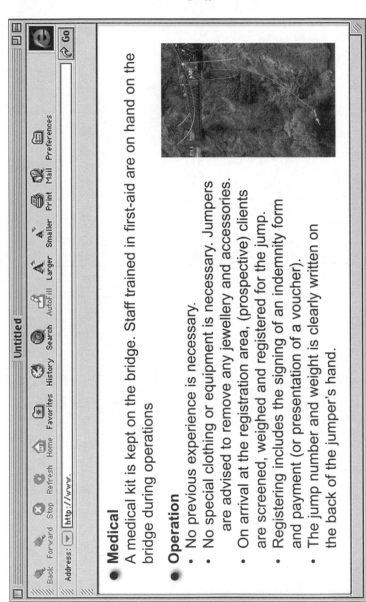

● Medical

A medical kit is kept on the bridge. Staff trained in first-aid are on hand on the bridge during operations

● Operation

- No previous experience is necessary.
- No special clothing or equipment is necessary. Jumpers are advised to remove any jewellery and accessories.
- On arrival at the registration area, (prospective) clients are screened, weighed and registered for the jump.
- Registering includes the signing of an indemnity form and payment (or presentation of a voucher).
- The jump number and weight is clearly written on the back of the jumper's hand.

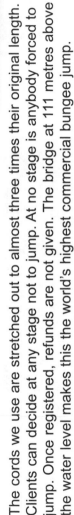

The jump

Prior to jumping, clients are briefed individually. This briefing includes: how the harness system works; the final jump procedure to be followed on the platform; what to expect during the jump; the recovery procedure.

The client is then harnessed up for the jump. All connections to the bungee cord are made before the jumper moves on to the platform. 5, 4, 3, 2, 1, BUNGEE...!!!

The cords we use are stretched out to almost three times their original length. Clients can decide at any stage not to jump. At no stage is anybody forced to jump. Once registered, refunds are not given. The bridge at 111 metres above the water level makes this the world's highest commercial bungee jump.

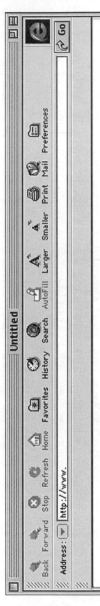

Back Forward Stop Refresh Home Favorites History Search AutoFill Larger Smaller Print Mail Preferences

Address: http://www.

● **Recovery system**

After the client has jumped, a recovery operator is lowered down to the jumper. The operator attaches a line to the mountaineering harness of the jumper, and the client then assumes an upright sitting position.

Both jumper and operator are then hoisted back up onto the catwalk below the bridge.

Clients are attached to a safety line on the catwalk and checked by a senior jumpmaster before being escorted to the top of the bridge.

Clients then return to the registration area to record their comments on the jump. A video recording of the jump can be seen immediately. Photographs of every jump are also available.

Tragedy

Nottingham Evening Post

Three newspaper reports tell the story of a boy who was killed by a train during a game of 'chicken'.

BOY, 12, KILLED IN RAIL HORROR

JAMES LEAVOLD and IAN DRURY

Friends watched in horror as a 12-year-old boy was struck by a 415-tonne freight train and killed.

Two boys jumped in front of the train at Toton Sidings, Stapleford, at around 6 last night.

One made it across the mainline track but his friend, a pupil at George Spencer School, Stapleford, was struck by the empty train that was approaching at 45mph.

Police were today questioning up to eight boys and girls who were trespassing on the track.

The driver of the train, that was pulling 11 wagons, braked when he saw the boys. The boy's family, who live in Toton, were 'absolutely devastated', police said.

Mr Saunders, a railway official, said today: 'The driver was clearly shaken by the incident. He suddenly saw the youngster but it was too late. A train like this takes several hundred yards for it to come to a stop.

'It just goes to show how dangerous railways can be'.

More than 300 people were killed on British railway lines last year.

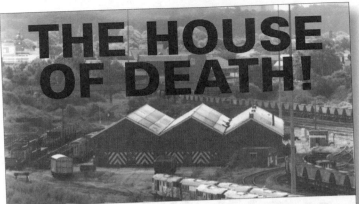

THE HOUSE OF DEATH!

Boy 'died in gang ritual'

IAN DRURY

A 12-year-old boy killed by a train is said to have been taking part in a gang ritual.

Shaun McGrath is believed to have been on the final part of the ritual when he was struck and killed by a 415-tonne goods train at Toton Sidings, near Stapleford.

A Railtrack investigation has uncovered evidence from children of an initiation ceremony. To become a gang member, children must complete three stages. They start by running across 16 railway lines to a building called the White House. As well as the risk of being hit by a train, they could be electrocuted. They then cross more lines to reach a building called the Black House. In the final stage, they must cross the depot's four main lines - including one used by high-speed commuter trains. They are heading for a disused building - called the House of Death.

Railtrack said today that children are still going through the ritual - less than a month after the tragedy.

A senior Railtrack source said: 'It is terrifying. They are playing Russian roulette just to join a gang.'

CHILDREN STILL RISKING THEIR LIVES

'Don't die like my son' plea

Ian Drury and David Whitfield

Just three months after 12-year-old Shaun McGrath was struck and killed by a goods train, transport police say children from the same school are continuing to trespass on the site.

The news has horrified Shaun's father Paul, who today pleaded with youngsters:

'After what happened to my lad, please keep off the railway.

'No-one wants to see another kid end up like Shaun. But I am worried the same thing is going to happen again. It is a terrible price to pay.

'These children don't know how much heartache it brings - and they don't want to know either.'

British Transport Police Constable Al Jones said: 'If anything was to come out of Shaun's accident, we would hope that it would be to stop other children risking their lives.

'But clearly, this is not happening. I find it irritating that these children have not learned from this tragedy.

'The maximum fine for trespassing on the railway is £1,000. But the maximum penalty is to lose your life.'

Activities

Moonies

1   As a group, discuss the following questions:

- Should Adam have agreed to carry out the dare?
- How could he have got out of doing the dare?
- Has anyone in the group ever got into trouble because of a dare?

2   Which characters do you like and which ones do you dislike in the story? Copy out and complete the two tables below. Write down the reasons for your decisions.

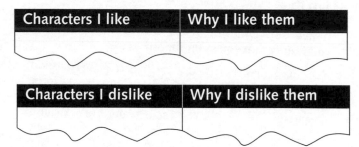

Characters I like	Why I like them

Characters I dislike	Why I dislike them

3   In chapter 3, Adam describes how he is feeling just before he does the moonie:

    'My fingers **were like jelly**.'

This is a **simile**. Adam's fingers are described as being like jelly in order to show:

- that they are shaking
- that he can't control them properly.

Find two more similes in chapter 3.

- What images come into your mind when you read these similes?
- Why do you think that the author, Paul Jennings, uses these similes?

Dare You

1 *Dare You* has an open ending – we cannot be certain what has happened to Jeanie.

Look at the final paragraph.
- What do you think has happened to Jeanie?
- Is she dead, asleep or unconscious?
- Are there any words or phrases that give any clues?

Write down what you think and give your reasons.

2 Does anyone in your group have a frightening tale to tell? Is it based on truth or is it just made up? Share your stories with each other.

3 *Dare You* has several elements in it that you would expect to find in many horror or ghost stories.

- Make a list of the things in the story that make it a 'typical' horror story. The list has been started for you:

> ○ Set at night
> ○ A group of children trying to scare each other
> ○ Squeaky gate
> ○

4 Using ideas from this list, write your own horror or ghost story.

5 In the first section of *Dare You*, there is a lot of dialogue (speech).

- Using this section, turn the story into a play script, which ends when Jeanie leaves the house. This is how the script should start:

    JEANIE: That's silly! What would it want to do that for?
    KEV: I don't know, but it does, anyway.

- When you have completed the script, get into threes and act it out. You could record it on audio or video tape.
- If you have the facilities and the time, you could even make this story into a film!

The History of Bungee Jumping

1   Look on the Internet or in the library to find out more information about Pentecostal Island. Use this information to make a fact file about the island:

  • where it is
  • how many people live there
  • what the climate is like
  • what crops are grown there, etc.

2   Re-read the extract and then answer the following questions. Remember to use full sentences in your answers.

  • In which ocean is Pentecostal Island?
  • Who was the first foreigner to make a jump on the island?
  • Where did the first bungee jump in the Western world take place?
  • Why did Pentecostal Islanders take part in the jumps?
  • How fast can a person's heart beat during a bungee jump?

3   What do the following words and phrases mean? Use a dictionary or reference books to help you.

  • terminal velocity
  • peer pressure
  • adrenalin
  • jungle vines

4   Use the Internet to find out more about bungee jumping. These two sites are good to begin with:

   http://www.BungeeZone.com/links
   http://www.greatsports.com/bungee

5   Now use any information you have obtained to write your own 'Bungee Jumping' fact file.

A Bungee Jump

1 Look in a world atlas to find out where Victoria Falls Bridge is. Then try to find pictures of Victoria Falls and the Victoria Falls Bridge at the library or in reference books.

2 Imagine you are going to do a bungee jump. Write a description of your jump, using the information from the extract to help you.

Remember to include:

- what you feel like before, during and after the jump
- what you are thinking
- what you can see and hear
- what other people think about you doing the jump.

3 Design a poster advertising a bungee jump. Use the information from the Shearwater advert to help you.

Think about what information and images you should include. Remember that you have to make it sound exciting, but not too scary!

You could use a computer to help you create the poster.

4 **Class survey**

Organise a class survey to find out how many people in your class would like to do a bungee jump.

- Find out their reasons for wanting to or not wanting to.
- Then present your findings to the rest of the class as a talk or as a wall display.

Tragedy

1   Work in small groups. Imagine you are a team of
     reporters for a radio station. Using the information from
     the newspaper articles, you have to produce a news
     report about the tragedy at Toton Sidings.

     Remember to include:

     •   details of what happened
     •   interviews with police, parents, gang members, etc
         (these should be played by different members of the
         group)
     •   a warning to other young people.

     Record your report on tape and play it to the rest of the
     class.

2   As a group, discuss the following questions:

     •   What does the phrase 'initiation ceremony' mean?
     •   Is anybody in your class in a gang?
     •   Has anybody had to do a dare to become a member
         of a gang?
     •   Why do people want to join gangs?

Comparing Texts

1   In small groups make up an improvisation entitled
    'DARE!'. You could base it on one or more of the texts in
    this section. Or you could base it on something that has
    happened to you or your friends.

    When you have practised it, act it out for the rest of the
    class.

2   Below is a list of words that could be used to describe
    being frightened.

    •   Start by putting them in order of intensity. The word
        that describes being *least* frightened should come
        first and the word that describes being the *most*
        frightened should be last.
    •   When you have finished, compare your list with
        those of other people in your group. Does everyone
        agree?

    > scared   jittery   uneasy   worried   terrified
    > petrified   dreading   alarmed   nervous
    > anxious   shaking   hysterical

3   **Group discussion**

    Both Adam in *Moonies* and the boy who was killed on
    the railway were taking part in a dare.

    As a group, discuss the following points:

    •   Why do people do dares?
    •   Could they say no? If not, why not?
    •   Why do people like to be scared?
    •   Is there a difference between daring to run across a
        railway track or daring to do a bungee jump?
    •   Has anybody done a dare that went wrong? What
        happened?

4 Write about your favourite extract from this section. Use a writing frame like the one below to help you.

Remember to include:

- why you like it
- the way it is written
- the subject matter
- what it makes you think or feel
- what other books or stories it reminds you of.

My favourite extract in this section is

....

I like it because

....

It also

....

It reminds me of

....

---

5 Now write about your *least* favourite extract, in a similar way.

My least favourite extract in this section is

....

I don't like it much because

....

I also think that it

....

Weird!

Spaghetti Pig-Out
Paul Jennings

Matthew's dad brings home a video remote control
with a difference – it works on people and animals!
Unfortunately Guts Garvey steals it. Can Matthew get
the gadget back and take his revenge?

1

Guts Garvey was a real mean kid. He made my life
miserable. I don't know why he didn't like me. I hadn't
done anything to him. Not a thing.

He wouldn't let any of the other kids hang around
with me. I was on my own. Anyone in the school who
spoke to me was in his bad books. I wandered around
the yard at lunch time like a dead leaf blown in
the wind.

I tried everything. I even gave him my pocket money
one week. He just bought a block of chocolate from
the canteen and ate it in front of me. Without even
giving me a bit. What a rat.

After school I only had one friend. My cat – Bad
Smell. She was called that because now and then she
would make a bad smell. Well, she couldn't help it.
Everyone has their faults. She was a terrific cat. But still.

A cat is not enough. You need other kids for friends too.

Even after school no one would come near me. I only had one thing to do. Watch the television. But that wasn't much good either. There were only little kids' shows on before tea.

'I wish we had a video,' I said to Mum one night.

'We can't afford it, Matthew,' said Mum. 'Anyway, you watch too much television as it is. Why don't you go and do something with a friend?'

I didn't say anything. I couldn't tell her that I didn't have any friends. And never would have as long as Guts Garvey was around. A bit later Dad came in. He had a large parcel under his arm. 'What have you got, Dad?' I asked.

'It's something good,' he answered. He put the package on the lounge-room floor and I started to unwrap it. It was about the size of a large cake. It was green and spongy with an opening in the front.

'What is it?' I said.

'What you've always wanted. A video player.'

I looked at it again. 'I've never seen a video player like this before. It looks more like a mouldy loaf of bread with a hole in the front.'

'Where did you get it?' asked Mum in a dangerous voice. 'And how much was it?'

'I bought it off a bloke in the pub. A real bargain. Only fifty dollars.'

'Fifty dollars is cheap for a video,' I said. 'But is it a video? It doesn't look like one to me. Where are the cables?'

'He said it doesn't need cables. You just put in the video and press this.' He handed me a green thing that looked like a bar of chocolate with a couple of licorice blocks stuck on the top.

'You're joking,' I said. 'That's not a remote control.'

'How much did you have to drink?' said Mum. 'You must have been crazy to pay good money for that junk.' She went off into the kitchen. I could tell that she was in a bad mood.

'Well, at least try it,' said Dad sadly. He handed me a video that he had hired down the street. It was called *Revenge of the Robots*. I pushed the video into the mushy hole and switched on the TV set. Nothing happened.

I looked at the licorice blocks on the green chocolate thing. It was worth a try. I pushed one of the black squares.

The movie started playing at once. 'It works,' I yelled. 'Good on you, Dad. It works. What a ripper.'

Mum came in and smiled. 'Well, what do you know,' she said. 'Who would have thought that funny-looking thing was a video set? What will they think of next?'

2

Dad went out and helped Mum get tea while I sat down and watched the movie. I tried out all the licorice-like buttons on the remote control. One was for fast forward, another was pause and another for rewind. The rewind was good. You could watch all the people doing things backwards.

I was rapt to have a video but to tell the truth the movie was a bit boring. I started to fiddle around with the handset. I pointed it at things in the room and pressed the buttons. I pretended that it was a ray gun.

'Tea time,' said Mum after a while.

'What are we having?' I yelled.

'Spaghetti,' said Mum.

I put the video on pause and went to the door. I was just about to say, 'I'm not hungry,' when I noticed something. Bad Smell was sitting staring at the TV in a funny way. I couldn't figure out what it was at first but I could see that something was wrong. She was so still. I had never seen a cat sit so still before. Her tail didn't swish. Her eyes didn't blink. She just sat there like a statue. I took off my thong and threw it over near her. She didn't move. Not one bit. Not one whisker.

'Dad,' I yelled. 'Something is wrong with Bad Smell.'

He came into the lounge and looked at the poor cat. It sat there staring up at the screen with glassy eyes. Dad waved his hand in front of her face. Nothing. Not a blink. 'She's dead,' said Dad.

'Oh no,' I cried. 'Not Bad Smell. Not her. She can't be. My only friend.' I picked her up. She stayed in the sitting-up position. I put her back on the floor. No change. She sat there stiffly. I felt for a pulse but I couldn't feel one. Her chest wasn't moving. She wasn't breathing.

'Something's not quite right,' said Dad. 'But I can't figure out what it is.'

'She shouldn't be sitting up,' I yelled. 'Dead cats don't sit up. They fall over with their legs pointed up.'

Dad picked up Bad Smell and felt all over her. 'It's no good, Matthew,' he said. 'She's gone. We will bury her in the garden after tea.' He patted me on the head and went into the kitchen.

Tears came into my eyes. I hugged Bad Smell to my chest. She wasn't stiff. Dead cats should be stiff. I remembered a dead cat that I once saw on the footpath. I had picked it up by the tail and it hadn't bent. It had been like picking up a saucepan by the handle.

Bad Smell felt soft. Like a toy doll. Not stiff and hard like the cat on the footpath.

Suddenly I had an idea. I don't know what gave it to me. It just sort of popped into my head. I picked up the funny-looking remote control, pointed it at Bad Smell and pressed the FORWARD button. The cat blinked, stretched, and stood up. I pressed PAUSE again and she froze. A statue again. But this time she was standing up.

I couldn't believe it. I rubbed my eyes. The pause button was working on my cat. I pressed FORWARD a second time and off she went. Walking into the kitchen as if nothing had happened.

Dad's voice boomed out from the kitchen 'Look. Bad Smell is alive.' He picked her up and examined her. 'She must have been in a coma. Just as well we didn't bury her.' Dad had a big smile on his face. He put Bad Smell down and shook his head. I went back to the lounge.

I hit one of the licorice-like buttons. None of them had anything written on them but by now I knew what each of them did.

Or I thought I did.

3

The movie started up again. I watched it for a while until a blow fly started buzzing around and annoying me. I pointed the hand set at it just for fun and pressed FAST FORWARD. The fly vanished. Or that's what seemed to happen. It was gone from sight but I could still hear it. The noise was tremendous. It was like a tiny jet fighter screaming around in the room. I saw something flash by. It whipped past me again. And again. And again. The blow fly was going so fast that I couldn't see it.

I pushed the PAUSE button and pointed it up where the noise was coming from. The fly must have gone right through the beam because it suddenly appeared out of nowhere. It hung silently in mid-air. Still. Solidified. A floating, frozen fly. I pointed the hand set at it again and pressed FORWARD. The blow fly came to life at once. It buzzed around the room at its normal speed.

'Come on,' yelled Mum. 'Your tea is ready.'

I wasn't interested in tea. I wasn't interested in anything except this fantastic remote control. It seemed to be able to make animals and insects freeze or go fast forward. I looked through the kitchen door at Dad. He had already started eating. Long pieces of spaghetti dangled from his mouth. He was chewing and sucking at the same time.

Now don't get me wrong. I love Dad. I always have. He is a terrific bloke. But one thing that he used to do really bugged me. It was the way he ate spaghetti. He sort of made slurping noises and the meat sauce gathered around his lips as he sucked. It used to get on my nerves. I think that's why I did what I did. I know it's a weak excuse. I shivered. Then I pointed the control at him and hit the PAUSE button.

Dad stopped eating. He turned rock solid and just sat there with the fork halfway up to his lips. His mouth was wide open. His eyes stared. The spaghetti hung from his fork like worms of concrete. He didn't blink. He didn't move. He was as stiff as a tree trunk.

Mum looked at him and laughed. 'Good one,' she said. 'You'd do anything for a laugh, Arthur.'

Dad didn't move.

'OK,' said Mum. 'That's enough. You're setting a bad example for Matthew by fooling around with your food like that.'

My frozen father never so much as moved an eyeball. Mum gave him a friendly push on the shoulder and he started to topple. Over he went. He looked just like a statue that had been pushed off its mount. Crash. He lay on the ground. His hand still halfway up to his mouth. The solid spaghetti hung in the same position. Only now it stretched out sideways pointing at his toes.

Mum gave a little scream and rushed over to him. Quick as a flash I pointed the remote control at him and pressed FORWARD. The spaghetti dangled downwards. Dad sat up and rubbed his head. 'What happened?' he asked.

'You had a little turn,' said Mum in a worried voice. 'You had better go straight down to the hospital and have a check up. I'll get the car. Matthew, you stay here and finish your tea. We won't be long.'

I was going to tell them about the remote control but something made me stop. I had a thought. If I told them about it they would take it off me. It was the last I would see of it for sure. If I kept it to myself I could take it to school. I could show Guts Garvey my fantastic new find. He would have to make friends with me now that I had something as good as this. Every kid in the school would want to have a go.

Dad and Mum came home after about two hours. Dad went straight to bed. The doctor had told him to have a few days' rest. He said Dad had been working too hard. I took the remote control to bed with me. I didn't use it until the next day.

4

It was Saturday and I slept in. I did my morning jobs and set out to find Guts Garvey. He usually hung around the shops on Saturday with his tough mates.

The shopping centre was crowded. As I went I looked in the shop windows. In a small café I noticed a man and a woman having lunch. They were sitting at a table close to the window. I could see everything that they were eating. The man was having a steak and what was left of a runny egg. He had almost finished his meal.

It reminded me of Dad and the spaghetti. I took out the remote control and looked at it. I knew that it could do PAUSE, FORWARD and FAST FORWARD. There was one more button. I couldn't remember what this last button was for. I pushed it.

I wouldn't have done it on purpose. I didn't really realise that it was pointing at the man in the shop. The poor thing.

The last button was REWIND.

Straight away he began to un-eat his meal. He went backwards. He put his fork up to his mouth and started taking out the food and placing it back on his plate. The runny egg came out of his mouth with bits of steak and chips. In, out, in, out, went his fork. Each time bringing a bit of food out of his mouth. He moved the mashed-up bits backwards on his plate with the knife and fork and they all formed up into solid chips, steak and eggs.

It was unbelievable. He was un-chewing his food and un-eating his meal. Before I could gather my wits his whole meal was back on the plate. He then put his clean knife and fork down on the table.

My head swirled but suddenly I knew what I had to do. I pressed FORWARD. Straight away he picked up his knife and fork and began to eat his meal for the second time. The woman sitting opposite him had pushed her fist up into her mouth. She was terrified. She didn't know what was going on. Suddenly she screamed and ran out of the café. The man didn't take any notice he just kept eating. He had to eat the whole meal again before he could stop.

I ran down the street feeling as guilty as sin. This thing was powerful. It could make people do things backwards.

I stopped at the corner. There, talking to his mean mate Rabbit, was Guts Garvey. This was my big chance to get into his good books. 'Look,' I said. 'Take a squizz at this.' I held out the remote control.

Guts Garvey grabbed it from my hand. 'Yuck,' he growled. 'Green chocolate. Buzz off, bird brain.' He lifted up the remote control. He was going to throw it at me.

'No,' I yelled. 'It's a remote control. From a video. You press the black things.' Guts Garvey looked at me. Then he looked at the control. He didn't believe me but he pressed one of the buttons.

Rabbit was bounding a basketball up and down on the footpath. He suddenly froze. So did the ball. Rabbit stood there on one leg and the ball floated without moving, halfway between his hand and the ground. Guts Garvey's mouth dropped open. He rubbed his eyes and looked again. The statue of Rabbit was still there.

'Press FORWARD,' I said, pointing to the top button.

Guts pressed the control and Rabbit finished bouncing the ball. I smiled. I could see that Guts was impressed. He turned and looked at me. Then he pointed the remote control straight at my face. 'No,' I screamed. 'No.'

But I was too late. Guts Garvey pressed the button. He 'paused' me. I couldn't move. I just stood there with both arms frozen up in the air. My eyes stared. They didn't move. Nothing moved. I was rock solid. Guts and Rabbit laughed. Then they ran off.

5

People gathered round. At first they laughed. A whole circle of kids and adults looking at the stupid dill standing there like a statue. Someone waved their hand in front of my face. A girl poked me. 'He's good,' said someone. 'He's not moving a muscle.'

I tried to speak. My mouth wouldn't move. My tongue wouldn't budge. The crowd got bigger. I felt an idiot. What a fool. Dozens of people were staring at me wondering why I was standing there posed like a picture on the wall. Then I stopped feeling stupid. I felt scared. What if I stayed like this forever? Not breathing. Not moving. Not alive, not dead. What would they do with me? Put me in the garden like a garden gnome? Stash me away in a museum? Bury me alive? It was too terrible to think about.

Suddenly I collapsed. I puddled onto the ground. Everyone laughed. I stood up and ran off as fast as I could go. As I ran I tried to figure it out. Why had I suddenly gone off pause? Then I realised what it was. I remembered my Uncle Frank's video. If you put it on pause and went away it would start up again automatically after three or four minutes. The movie would come off pause and keep going. That's what had happened to me.

I looked ahead. I could just make out two tiny figures in the distance. It was Rabbit and Guts Garvey. With my remote control. I had to get it back. The dirty rats had nicked it. I didn't care about getting in Guts Garvey's good books any more. I just wanted my controller back.

And revenge. I wanted revenge.

I ran like a mad thing after them.

It was no good. I was out of breath and they were too far away. I couldn't catch them. I looked around. Shaun Potter, a kid from school, was sitting on his horse, Star, on the other side of the road. I rushed over to him. 'Help,' I said. 'You've got to help. Guts Garvey has pinched my remote control. I've got to get it back. It's a matter of life and death.'

Shaun looked at me. He wasn't a bad sort of kid. He was one of the few people in the school who had been kind to me. He wasn't exactly a friend. He was too scared of Guts Garvey for that. But I could tell by the way he smiled and nodded at me that he liked me. I jumped from foot to foot. I was beside myself. I had to get that remote control back. Shaun hesitated for a second or two. Then he said, 'OK, hop up.'

I put one foot in the stirrup and Shaun pulled me up behind him onto Star's back. 'They went that way,' I yelled.

Star went into a trot and then a canter. I held on for grim death. I had never been on a horse before. I bumped up and down behind Shaun. The ground seemed a long way down. I was scared but I didn't say anything. I had to catch Guts Garvey and Rabbit. We sped down the street past all the parked cars and people crossing the road.

'There they are,' I yelled. Guts and Rabbit were in a line of people waiting for a bus. Shaun slowed Star down to a walk. Guts Garvey looked up and saw us. He pulled the remote control from his pocket. 'Oh no,' I yelled. 'Not that.'

6

I don't know whether or not Star sensed danger. Anyway, he did what horses often do at such times. He lifted up his tail and let a large steaming flow of horse droppings fall onto the road. Then he took a few steps towards Guts and the line of people.

Guts pointed the remote control at us and hit the REWIND button. 'Stop,' I screamed. But it was too late. Star began to go into reverse. She walked a few steps backwards. The pile of horse droppings began to stir. It twisted and lifted. Then it flew through the air – back to where it came from.

The line of people roared. Some laughed. Some screamed. Some ran off. How embarrassing. I was filled with shame. Poor Star went into a backwards trot. Then, suddenly she froze. We all froze. Guts had hit the PAUSE button. He had turned Shaun, Star and me into statues.

While we were standing there like stiff dummies the bus pulled up. All the people in the queue piled on. They couldn't get on quickly enough. They wanted to get away from the mad boys and their even madder horse.

After four or five minutes the pause effect wore off. We were able to move. I climbed down off Star's back. 'Sorry,' I said to Shaun. 'I didn't know that was going to happen.'

Shaun stared down at me. He looked pale. 'I think I've just had a bad dream,' he said. 'In the middle of the day. I think I'd better go home.' He shook his head slowly and then trotted off.

7

'Rats,' I said to myself. Everything was going wrong. I had lost the remote control. Guts Garvey had nicked it and there was nothing I could do about it. I was too scared to go near him in case he put me into reverse again. I felt terrible. I walked home with slow, sad footsteps.

When I got home Dad was mad because the remote control had disappeared. I couldn't tell him what had happened. He would never believe it. I had to spend most of the weekend pretending to help him look for it. The video wouldn't work without the control.

On Monday it was back to school as usual. Back to wandering around with no one to talk to.

As I walked around the schoolyard my stomach rumbled. I was hungry. Very hungry. I hadn't had anything to eat since tea time on Friday night. The reason for this was simple. This was the day of The Great Spaghetti Pig-out. A competition to see who could eat the most spaghetti bolognaise in fifteen minutes.

The grand final was to be held in the school hall. The winner received a free trip to London for two and the entrance money went to charity. I had a good chance of winning. Even though I was skinny I could eat a lot when I was hungry. I had won all the heats. My record was ten bowls of spaghetti bolognaise in fifteen minutes. Maybe if I won the competition I would also win the respect of the kids. I was going to give the tickets to London to Mum and Dad. They needed a holiday badly.

I didn't see Guts Garvey until just before the competition. He kept out of my sight all day. I knew he was cooking up some scheme but I didn't know what it was.

There were four of us up on the platform. Me, two girls and Guts Garvey. The hall was packed with kids and teachers. I felt confident but nervous. I knew that I could win. I looked at Guts Garvey and saw that he was grinning his head off. Then I saw Rabbit in the front row. His pocket was bulging. Rabbit had something in his pocket and I thought I knew what it was.

They were up to no good. Guts and Rabbit had something cooked up and it wasn't spaghetti.

The plates of steaming spaghetti bolognaise were lined up in front of us. Everything was ready for the starter to say 'go'. My empty stomach was in a knot. My mind was spinning. I tried to figure out what they were up to. What if I ate five plates of spaghetti and Rabbit put me into reverse? I would un-eat it like the man in the café. I would go backwards and take all of the spaghetti out and put it back on the plate. My knees started to knock.

I decided to back out of the competition. I couldn't go through with it.

'Go,' yelled Mr Stepney, the school principal. It was too late. I had to go on.

I started shovelling spaghetti into my mouth. There was no time to mix in the meat sauce. I just pushed in the platefuls as they came. One, two, three. The winner would be the one to eat the most plates in fifteen minutes.

I watched Guts and the others out of the corner of my eye. I was already ahead by two bowls. In, out, in, out. Spaghetti, spaghetti, spaghetti. I was up to seven bowls, Guts had eaten only four and the two girls had managed two each. I was going to win. Mum and Dad would be pleased.

Rabbit was watching us from the front row. I noticed Guts nod to him. Rabbit took something out of his pocket. I could see that it was the remote control. He was going to put me on rewind. I was gone.

But no. Rabbit was not pointing the control at me. He pointed it at Guts. What was going on? I soon found out. Guts began eating the spaghetti at enormous speed. Just like a movie on fast forward. His fork went up and down to his mouth so quickly that you could hardly see it. He licked like lightning. He swallowed at top speed. Boy did he go. His arms whirled. The spaghetti flew. Ten, eleven, twelve bowls. Thirteen, fourteen, fifteen. He was plates ahead. I didn't have a chance to catch up to Guts the guzzling gourmet. He fed his face like a whirlwind. It was incredible. Inedible. But it really happened.

Rabbit had put Guts on FAST FORWARD so that he would eat more plates than me in the fifteen minutes. It wasn't fair. But there was nothing I could do.

The audience cheered and shouted. They thought that Guts was fantastic. No one had ever seen anything like it before. He was up to forty bowls. I had only eaten ten and the two girls six each. The siren blew. Guts was the winner. I was second.

He had eaten forty bowls. No one had ever eaten forty bowls of spaghetti before. Rabbit hit FORWARD on the control and Guts stopped eating. Everyone cheered Guts. I looked at my shoes. I felt ill and it wasn't just from eating ten plates of spaghetti. I swallowed. I had to keep it all down. That was one of the rules – you weren't allowed to be sick. If you threw up you lost the competition.

8

Guts stood up. He looked a bit funny. His face was a green colour. His stomach swelled out over his belt. He started to sway from side to side. Then he opened his mouth.

Out it came. A great tumbling, surge of spew. A tidal wave of swallowed spaghetti and meat sauce. It flowed down the table and onto the floor. A brown and white lake of sick. Guts staggered and tottered. He lurched to the edge of the stage. He opened his mouth again and let forth another avalanche. The kids in the front row screamed as the putrid waterfall splashed down. All over Rabbit.

Rabbit shrieked and sent the remote control spinning into the air. I jumped forward and grabbed it.

I shouldn't have done what I did. But I couldn't help myself. I pointed the control at Guts and the river of sick.

Then I pressed REWIND.

9

After that Guts Garvey was not very popular at school. To say the least. But I had lots of friends. And Mum and Dad had a great time in London.

And as to what happened to the remote control . . . Well. That's another story.

At the Zoo
Brian Patten

Class 10XA visit the zoo and study two newly arrived creatures in a cage. But what type of creatures are they?

Two new creatures had arrived at the zoo, and Class 10XA were clustered around the cage, studying them.

'Don't go so near the cage,' said the teacher.

'They don't look dangerous,' said one of the pupils.

'They look sweet,' said another.

'They might look sweet,' said the teacher, 'but that's because they are young, and even the young ones are known to be quite vicious at times. They are carnivorous from a very early age, remember.'

'What's carnivorous?' asked one of the pupils.

'It means they eat meat.'

'Does that mean they would eat us?'

'Quite possibly,' said the teacher.

'They look tame,' said another pupil. 'They've hardly moved since we came.'

'That's because they are more interested in the box in the corner of their cage than in us, I suspect,' said the teacher.

'If you put one of those boxes in front of them, they will sit still for hours. It's when you take the box away that they go a bit wild.'

'Well, I think they are very sweet,' said one of the class. 'They look slightly like the monkeys in the other cage. Are they as intelligent?'

'Oh, no,' said the teacher. 'They can't do half the things the monkeys can.'

'I think they are quite boring myself,' said another of the pupils, 'and all that pink skin – yuk! They're so ugly!'

'Maybe they'd be more interesting if they weren't gaping at that box,' said the teacher. 'But they do move about, usually in the daylight. Anyway, they are part of our zoo project, and you must all use your computer note-pads to describe them.'

Class 10XA soon got bored looking at the new arrivals and moved along to another cage.

As they drifted away, one of the pupils asked, 'Where did you say they came from?'

'I've already told you,' said the teacher. 'Honestly, Harsog! Sometimes I think you've no brains in any of your three heads! They are from a planet called Earth, and they are called children. Now, don't let me have to tell you again!'

Spontaneous Human Combustion
Herbie Brennan

Can people really burst into flames? Read on and find out . . .

If it's chilly outside and you're wondering how on earth to get warm, thank your lucky stars you haven't (yet) experienced one of the most terrifying weirdnesses ever to face the human race . . .

WALES, 1980

Human beings have been bursting into flames for no reason that can be seen throughout history.

This scary phenomenon is known as SHC (Spontaneous Human Combustion). Some people don't believe in it but several cases in recent years have forced scientists to look at the grisly evidence again.

One of the leading UK investigators of SHC is John Heymer, a retired officer with Gwent CID. He is not easily fooled and assesses facts with the greatest care. Some fascinating case studies that he has collected have convinced him that Spontaneous Human Combustion is seriously real.

On 6 January 1980, for example, Heymer was called to the scene of a fire in a house in

Ebbw Vale, South Wales. He describes entering a living room lit by a strange orange-red glow. The room was radiating warmth and both the window and the light bulb were covered in a sticky orange-red substance. Greasy soot covered the walls and ceiling.

The knobs on the TV were melted and there were ashes from a coal fire in the grate. A partly burnt armchair was beside the fire and on the floor in between were the trousered remains of a leg and two feet at one end and a blackened skull at the other, surrounded by a great deal of ash. These tragic remains, all that was left of 73-year-old Henry Thomas, lay on a fitted carpet and part of the hearth rug. Both were charred only where they were touched by the ashes of the body.

Normal cases of death by fire burn from the outside in. But in the case of Henry Thomas, the fire appeared to have started from the inside out. Like a bonfire, the fire eventually burnt out, leaving part of his legs and feet.

Nothing else in the room had caught fire. The room itself was so well sealed that the oxygen supply had been quickly used up. As far as science is concerned, nothing can burn without oxygen, so the fire could only have lasted a short time. The lack of oxygen makes the burning of Mr Thomas's body even more mysterious. Just about everything else in the room should have burnt more easily than his body.

Even more weird was the fact that the ordinary plastic floor tiles beneath the carpet were completely undamaged, while most of the body on the carpet was reduced to ashes.

Despite the strangeness of the case, forensic experts preferred to believe that Mr Thomas had fallen head first into the grate, set fire to his head, then sat back down in his chair and waited quietly to burn to death. This was how they actually wrote their report, despite the fact that there was no evidence Mr Thomas had fallen into the fire at all.

An inquest later suggested that the fire had been a routine accident probably caused by a spark or a dropped cigarette. Mr Thomas was a non-smoker.

FACT FILE

1. The human body is about 70 per cent water. The average person contains about 170 litres of fluid. It is hardly possible that a body could burn all the way through at all.

2. Spontaneous Human Combustion is far from new. A search through historical records shows that it was known in the Middle Ages and even as far back as ancient Greece and Rome. Back then it was believed to be caused supernaturally by 'fire from heaven'.

3. In Victorian Britain, three friends were out for a seaside walk when the one in the middle suddenly burst into a pillar of flame. He burnt so fiercely that his companions were unable to approach him, let alone help. This is one of the very few cases where SHC occurred in the presence of witnesses.

4. It seems that water does not work against SHC, but the fire can apparently be smothered if action is taken quickly enough. In one case study, the victim reported a small blue flame that leaped without warning out of his arm and burned fiercely, although without giving him pain. Instinctively he clamped his hand over it . . . and the fire went out.

What are Black Holes?
Hazel Richardson

Explore black holes, red giants and white dwarfs, some of the wonders of the universe. There is also an experiment which is guaranteed to go with a bang!

Black holes are the strangest and most terrifying things in the universe. We know that they are out there, but we can't see them because they are so black – blacker than the darkest place you have ever been in. Amazingly, they start off as stars brighter than the Sun.

FROM RED GIANT TO WHITE DWARF OR BLACK HOLE?
Many new stars are enormous, with enough fuel to burn for millions of years, even though they burn millions of tonnes of fuel every second. (In smaller stars like our Sun, the fuel can last for billions of years!) If we wait for a few million years and then return to the star we watched being born, we can see what happens when it starts to run out of fuel.

Most of the hydrogen in the star has been turned into helium, so it starts fusing together helium atoms instead of hydrogen. This makes heavier atoms like carbon and iron. The star carries on burning happily for a few more million years, but eventually, even the helium runs out. Now the star is in big trouble – the force of gravity begins to take over.

The birth of a star

Space, a few billion years ago

Here we are, surrounded by floating clouds of hot gas left over from the Big Bang. The gas is made up of hydrogen, and the atoms in it bump into each other and stick together. This makes a spinning ball of gas, which gets bigger and bigger and heavier and heavier. The atoms in the centre of the ball get squeezed together and the pressure makes them heat up.

The centre of the ball of gas eventually reaches over 15 million °C! When it gets this hot, the hydrogen atoms have enough energy to join together and turn into helium atoms. This is called nuclear fusion and it releases an enormous amount of energy as heat and light. A star is born!

Gravity is the pulling force that keeps us on the ground. The heavier something is, the greater the force of gravity it has. (For instance, the Moon is a lot smaller and lighter than the Earth, so it has one-sixth of the gravity of Earth.) As the star burns helium and makes heavier elements, the centre of it gets heavier and heavier and the gravity inside gets stronger.

The gravity squeezes the centre of the star so hard that it gets even hotter. The outside of the star billows out to an enormous size and the star becomes what is called a red giant.

Smaller stars, like our Sun, turn into red giants and then shrink into tiny, cool stars called white dwarves. (This will happen to our Sun in about another 5 billion years. It will eventually end up about the same size as the Earth.)

But if it's a really massive star that has become a red giant, something even more spectacular happens. The star has burnt up all its fuel and is only left with iron inside it, which can't be used for nuclear fusion. To get the energy to try and fuse the iron together it tries to squeeze its centre more and the result is disaster! Within a few seconds the temperature inside the star shoots up to the unbelievable level of 50 billion °C and the star is ripped apart! The explosion is as bright as a billion suns and is called a supernova.

Astronomers actually watched a star explode like this about 300 years ago. The cloud of dust it threw off is called Cassiopeia A, and it can still be seen today.

Ursa Major
(The Plough)

the Pole Star

Cepheus

Cassiopeia A

Orion

North

When a really massive star is ripped apart like this, the core of the star is left behind, but gravity within it is so strong that not even light can escape from its surface. Nothing can prevent the core collapsing in under its own gravity, and it turns into a black hole.

Black holes are usually only made when a star weighs more than three times as much as the Sun. Can you imagine how gigantic these stars are? And a star that is 2 million kilometres across can be squeezed to only a couple of kilometres across! All the mass in the centre being squeezed so tightly into such a small space makes the force of gravity enormous.

**Be a time-travelling scientist –
SEE HOW BEING SQUEEZED CAN
MAKE A STAR EXPLODE**

WARNING
This is a REALLY messy experiment – so ask
permission first.

WHAT YOU'LL NEED
- an orange (this is your
  pretend star)
- a clamp
- something to clamp
  your orange to

WHAT TO DO
1 Clamp your pretend
  orange star to a table or
  other surface.
2 Slowly turn the clamp tighter and tighter
  and tighter.
3 Watch what happens.

WHAT HAPPENS?
The orange explodes. Happy cleaning!

Urban Myths
Rick Glanvill and Phil Healey

Urban myths are like jokes – we don't know who starts them, but they spread like wildfire! They might or might not be true, but urban myths are certainly some of the weirdest and most gruesome stories in the world . . .

Gone to seed

A boy sat down for breakfast one morning. His mum started to have a go at him.

'How many times have I told you to wipe your nose?' she said.

The boy was not surprised that his mum was telling him off – that happened all the time. But he was sure that his nose was not runny.

'My nose is clean, Mum,' said the boy. 'I just washed my face . . . honest!'

But his mum did not believe him. She said she could see the dirt under his nose for herself. So she did what mums always do. She picked up a tissue, spat on it, and started to rub away at her son's nose. To her amazement, it wasn't the usual yucky stuff. It was a little green leaf sticking out of his nostril!

She was horrified. She saw that the leaf was attached to a stem, and the stem went right up inside her son's nose. She rushed him to the hospital. Nurses looked at the leaf and decided the boy needed an operation right away.

An hour later, a doctor came over to the boy's mum. He told her that the operation had gone well.

'But what was wrong, doctor?' she asked.

'It was very strange,' said the doctor. 'Your son must have sneezed when he was eating a tomato. One of the tomato seeds got stuck at the top of his nose and began to grow.'

'We had to remove the tomato plant, or else it would have grown right up into your son's brain.'

Super fly guy

A young man had just started his first job. He was an assistant in a fishing tackle shop. He was a hard worker, and soon he was looking after the shop on his own.

One week his boss said that he would be going away for a long weekend. The young assistant would have to lock up the shop on Saturday, and open it again on Monday morning.

After a busy Saturday, the lad turned the sign on the door round to CLOSED. Then he swept up and turned off all the switches.

On Monday morning he arrived early to open up the shop. He pulled back the shutters, unlocked the door and checked the till.

The first customer of the day wanted some maggots. So the assistant popped round to the back of the shop to get a tub of them from the cold store.

When he opened the heavy door of the cold store, he knew that he shouldn't have turned off the fridge, because a huge cloud of bluebottles flew straight at him. The flies swarmed right into his mouth, and he choked to death.

Activities

Spaghetti Pig-Out

1   Make a list of all the things that happen in each chapter of the story. Write in note form, not full sentences. Use these notes on the first chapter as your model.

> <u>Chapter 1</u> – Matthew explains about Guts Garvey & why he has no friends except Bad Smell. Explains he wants video. Dad brings odd-looking video home – Mum angry – Matthew tries video – it works.

2   Imagine a member of your family, or a friend, doing something that annoys you. Imagine you have Matthew's video control and can 'Pause' them.

   •   Write a description of the still picture you would see. Try to make your description as vivid and interesting as possible, as Matthew does when he describes his Dad 'paused' while eating spaghetti (pages 152–153).

3   What would happen if you were sent into 'Rewind' mode just after you'd got up?

   •   Write down in the form of a list everything you do when you get up in the morning. Make it as detailed as possible.
   •   Now rewrite this list, but in reverse order! Your piece of writing should now describe how you 'get up' backwards!

4 Where do you think the video remote control might have come from? Write an advertisement for the 'Lost and Found' section of a newspaper, which explains:

- what the 'video' really is (or what it does besides play video tapes)
- who its original owner is
- how it came to be lost
- what reward is being offered for its return.

5 From the description given in the story (chapter 1, pages 148–149) draw a picture of the remote control and the video player it is supposed to operate. Use this in your advertisement.

At the Zoo

1   What do you think the 'box in the corner of the cage' is?
    (pages 164–165). Why do the zoo 'animals' go wild
    when it is taken away?

2   The alien teacher clearly thinks that the monkeys in the
    next cage are more intelligent than the 'animals' its class
    are studying. Why do you think the teacher has come to
    this conclusion?

3   Draw a picture of the alien teacher, using any clues you
    can find in the story to help you.

4   Below your drawing, write your own description of the
    alien teacher and try to imagine:

    •   what subjects it teaches
    •   the class's nickname for it
    •   its hobbies.

5   An alien might have no idea of, for instance, what hair is
    or what it is for. It might make the wrong assumptions –
    for example, that a person's clothing is part of its skin.

    •   Imagine you are an alien. Write a description of a
        human being. Make your description as detailed and
        vivid as you can; remember, you are writing for an
        audience of aliens who have never seen a human
        before.

Spontaneous Human Combustion

1   Answer the following questions, remembering to use full sentences in your answers.

- What does SHC stand for?
- What did John Heymer find on the evening of 6 January 1980?
- What did forensic experts believe had happened to Henry Thomas?
- How much water does the average human body contain?
- What was SHC thought to be caused by in ancient Greece and Rome?

2   Read the extract again and then complete the following newspaper report.

South Wales Post   *7 January 1980*

Up in smoke!

Scientists were baffled yesterday by the death of an Ebbw Vale man called, _____ .

The remains of the 73-year-old were discovered lying on _____ near _____ .

The window and the light bulb were coated with _____ . There was also damage to a _____ , and _____ , as well as to the parts of the carpet touched by ashes from the body.

Apart from the victim's blackened skull, only his _____ were found; the rest of his body was reduced to ash. This is mysterious because _____ _____ .

Experts say that the victim may have _____ _____, but this theory is unlikely because there is no evidence to suggest that _____ _____ .

What are Black Holes?

The diagram below describes what happens to stars to cause them to become black holes. Fill in the missing information in the boxes below.

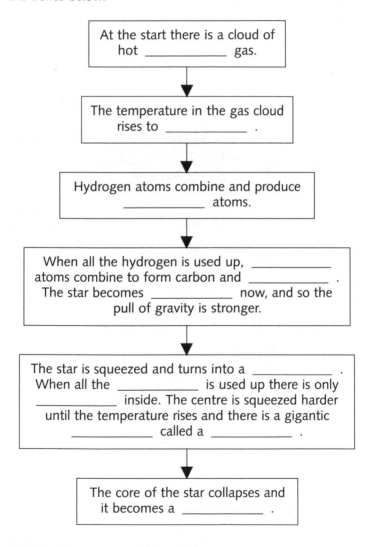

At the start there is a cloud of hot _____ gas.

The temperature in the gas cloud rises to _____ .

Hydrogen atoms combine and produce _____ atoms.

When all the hydrogen is used up, _____ atoms combine to form carbon and _____ . The star becomes _____ now, and so the pull of gravity is stronger.

The star is squeezed and turns into a _____ . When all the _____ is used up there is only _____ inside. The centre is squeezed harder until the temperature rises and there is a gigantic _____ called a _____ .

The core of the star collapses and it becomes a _____ .

Urban Myths

1   The conversations in the first myth on pages 175–176
    are written in **direct speech**. The boy's mum is the first
    to speak:

> *'How many times have I told you to wipe your
> nose?' she said.*

If this remark were written in **reported speech**, it would
appear like this:

> *She asked her son how many times she had told him
> to wipe his nose.*

- Rewrite each of the sentences below in **reported speech**.

    a   'My nose is clean, Mum,' said the boy. 'I just
        washed my face . . .honest.'
    b   'But what was wrong, doctor?' she asked.
    c   'It was very strange,' said the doctor. 'Your son
        must have sneezed when he was eating a tomato.'

2   Do you think these are true stories? Divide a piece of lined
    paper into two columns, with the following headings:

This story may be true because	This story may not be true because

- For each story, give two or three reasons for
  believing it to be true and two or three reasons for
  thinking it to be false. Discuss your findings with a
  partner.

3   Do you know any 'urban myths' like these? If so, tell
    them to your group. Do you believe they are true stories
    that really happened?

Comparing Texts

1 Group debate

This section of the book has dealt with strange and unlikely phenomena:

- Spontaneous Human Combustion
- alien life forms
- time travel via black holes, etc.

a Choose one of these phenomena, or any other interesting supernatural phenomenon, for example:

- ghosts and life after death
- monsters and strange beasts (Nessie, the Yeti, Bigfoot etc)
- the power of the pyramids and the curse of the Pharaohs
- the Bermuda Triangle

and find out as much information as you can. Look for evidence that has led people to believe that this phenomenon exists and make some notes.

b Explain the phenomenon you have chosen to your group. Be prepared to argue either:

- that the phenomenon does exist, and the evidence you have gathered demonstrates this **or**
- that the phenomenon does *not* exist and that the evidence for its existence can be explained away **or**
- that there is evidence for and against the phenomenon, and you are not sure whether it exists or not.

When all the presentations have been made, take a vote to see how many people in the group believe in each of the phenomena discussed. Which phenomenon is the most widely believed? and which the least?

2 What type of book would you be most likely to find these extracts in? Copy out and complete the table below. Some extracts will have more than one tick.

Where you would find them	Spaghetti	At Zoo	SHC	Black Holes	Gone to Seed	Super Fly Guy
Book of comedy stories						
Collection of sci-fi stories						
Book about the unexplained						
Science textbook						
Collection of weird stories						
Collection of true stories						
Newspaper						
Book of adventure stories						

ALSO IN

Heinemann
New Windmills

Founding Editors: Anne and Ian Serraillier

Chinua Achebe Things Fall Apart
David Almond Skellig
Maya Angelou I Know Why the Caged Bird Sings
Margaret Atwood The Handmaid's Tale
Jane Austen Pride and Prejudice
J G Ballard Empire of the Sun
Stan Barstow Joby; A Kind of Loving
Nina Bawden Carrie's War; Devil by the Sea; Kept in the Dark; The
Finding; Humbug
Lesley Beake A Cageful of Butterflies
Malorie Blackman Tell Me No Lies; Words Last Forever
Martin Booth Music on the Bamboo Radio
Ray Bradbury The Golden Apples of the Sun; The Illustrated Man
Betsy Byars The Midnight Fox; The Pinballs; The Not-Just-Anybody
Family; The Eighteenth Emergency
Victor Canning The Runaways
Jane Leslie Conly Racso and the Rats of NIMH
Robert Cormier We All Fall Down
Roald Dahl Danny, The Champion of the World; The Wonderful
Story of Henry Sugar; George's Marvellous Medicine; The BFG;
The Witches; Boy; Going Solo; Matilda; My Year
Anita Desai The Village by the Sea
Charles Dickens A Christmas Carol; Great Expectations;
Hard Times; Oliver Twist; A Charles Dickens Selection
Peter Dickinson Merlin Dreams
Berlie Doherty Granny was a Buffer Girl; Street Child
Roddy Doyle Paddy Clarke Ha Ha Ha
Anne Fine The Granny Project
Jamila Gavin The Wheel of Surya
Graham Greene The Third Man and The Fallen Idol; Brighton Rock
Thomas Hardy The Withered Arm and Other Wessex Tales
L P Hartley The Go-Between
Ernest Hemmingway The Old Man and the Sea; A Farewell to Arms
Frances Mary Hendry Chandra
Barry Hines A Kestrel For A Knave
Nigel Hinton Getting Free; Buddy; Buddy's Song; Out of the
Darkness
Anne Holm I Am David

Janni Howker Badger on the Barge; The Nature of the Beast; Martin Farrell
Pete Johnson The Protectors
Jennifer Johnston Shadows on Our Skin
Geraldine Kaye Comfort Herself
Daniel Keyes Flowers for Algernon
Clive King Me and My Million
Dick King-Smith The Sheep-Pig
Elizabeth Laird Red Sky in the Morning; Kiss the Dust
D H Lawrence The Fox and The Virgin and the Gypsy; Selected Tales
George Layton The Swap
Harper Lee To Kill a Mockingbird
Julius Lester Basketball Game
C Day Lewis The Otterbury Incident
Joan Lingard Across the Barricades; The File on Fraulein Berg
Penelope Lively The Ghost of Thomas Kempe
Jack London The Call of the Wild; White Fang
Bernard MacLaverty Cal; The Best of Bernard Mac Laverty
Margaret Mahy The Haunting
Anthony Masters Wicked
James Vance Marshall Walkabout
Ian McEwan The Daydreamer; A Child in Time
Pat Moon The Spying Game
Michael Morpurgo My Friend Walter; The Wreck of the Zanzibar; The War of Jenkins' Ear; Why the Whales Came; Arthur, High King of Britain
Beverley Naidoo No Turning Back
Bill Naughton The Goalkeeper's Revenge
New Windmill A Charles Dickens Selection
New Windmill Book of Classic Short Stories
New Windmill Book of Fiction and Non-fiction: Taking Off!
New Windmill Book of Haunting Tales
New Windmill Book of Humorous Stories: Don't Make Me Laugh
New Windmill Book of Nineteenth Century Short Stories
New Windmill Book of Non-fiction: Get Real!
New Windmill Book of Non-fiction: Real Lives, Real Times
New Windmill Book of Scottish Short Stories
New Windmill Book of Short Stories: Fast and Curious
New Windmill Book of Short Stories: Tales with a Twist

How many have you read?